Making Sense of Drama

A Guide to Classroom Practice

Jonothan Neelands

Advisory Teacher for English and Drama
Northamptonshire

Heinemann Educational Books

Published in association with 2D Magazine

Heinemann Educational Books Ltd
Halley Court, Jordan Hill, Oxford OX2 8EJ

OXFORD LONDON EDINBURGH
MADRID ATHENS BOLOGNA PARIS
MELBOURNE SYDNEY AUCKLAND SINGAPORE TOKYO
IBADAN NAIROBI HARARE GABORONE
PORTSMOUTH NH (USA)

British Library Cataloguing in Publication Data

Neelands, Jonothan
 Making sense of drama: a guide to classroom practice.
 1. Drama – Study and teaching
 I. Title
 792'.07'1   PN1701

ISBN 0-435-18658-2

First published 1984
91 92 93 94 95   15 14 13 12 11 10 9 8 7 6

For Eileen, Leo and Topsy (and all the lost weekends!)

Printed and bound in Great Britain by
Biddles Ltd, Guildford and King's Lynn

Contents

Acknowledgements

This book started life as *A Drama Handbook*, an in-service document prepared for Northamptonshire teachers on L E A drama courses. It owes its present form to the encouragement and advice of Ken Byron, Chris Lawrence and David Jackson. As I write, the ideas change and develop; the book represents a stage in a long and continuing cycle of growth; *it is not an orthodoxy* – it is a contribution.

Writing it down has helped and accelerated my own attempts at making sense of drama; I hope that reading it works in the same way for you.

Although this book represents a personal and particular view of drama, it would be unfair not to mention the sources and influences that have developed and shaped that view.

The following people have been closely involved with the shaping of many of the ideas contained in this book: Bill Shaw, Jane Bowden, Stephanie Key, Neill Kitson, Simon Bannister, Frances Bannister, David Clark, Paul Stanton, George Cockcroft, Peter Woods. I am also grateful for the valuable discussions I've shared with many other teachers on residential, evening and after-school courses.

Much of the thinking behind the book was firmed up and clarified by listening and talking with:

Dorothy Heathcote – Lecturer in Drama, University of Newcastle-upon-Tyne
Gavid Bolton – Lecturer in Drama, University of Durham
Geoff Gillham – Freelance Young People's Theatre worker
Geoff Readman – Inspector for Drama, Nottinghamshire
Deirdre Griffin – Leader, Brycbox Arts Centre
Robert Staunton – Advisory Teacher for Drama, Leicestershire
Cecily O'Neill – Warden, ILEA Tape and Drama Centre
Ken Byron – Advisory Teacher for Drama, Leicestershire
Chris Lawrence – Advisory Teacher for Drama, Newcastle-upon-Tyne
David Davies – Lecturer in Drama, Birmingham Polytechnic
Rosemary Linnell – Advisory Teacher for Drama, ILEA.

Finally, I am indebted to Vicki Snook for her help with the typing and the diagrams.

FURTHER READING

The following books and periodicals have been crucial to my own development as a drama practitioner.

ARMSTRONG, M. (1981) *Closely Observed Children* (Writers and Readers)
BOLTON, G. (1982) *Drama and the Emotions* (Unpublished)
BOLTON, G. (1981) Drama in the curriculum *2D* 1, 1
BOLTON, G. (1980) *Towards a Theory of Drama in Education* (Longman)
BYRON, K. (1983) Infant drama *2D* 2, 2 and 3
BRUNER, J., JOLLY, H. and SYLVA, (eds) (1976) *Play: Its Role in Development and Evolution* (Penguin)
COURTNEY, R. (1981) *The Dramatic Curriculum* (Heinemann Educational)
DAVIES, G. (1983) *Practical Primary Drama* (Heinemann Educational)
DONALDSON, M. (1976) *Children's Minds* (Fontana)
ELAM, K. (1980) *The Semiotics of Theatre and Drama* (Methuen)
HEATHCOTE, D. (1981) Material for meaning in drama *London Drama* 6, 2
HEATHCOTE, D. (1982) Signs and portents *SCYPT Journal* 9
ILEA ADVISORY TEACHERS (1977) *Drama Guidelines* (Heinemann Educational)
JACKSON, D. (1982) *Continuity in Secondary English* (Methuen)
KEMPE, A. (1982) Social drama *2D* 1, 3
LAWRENCE, C. (1982) Teacher and role *2D* 1, 2
LINELL, R. (1982) *Approaching Classroom Drama* (Arnold)
McENTEGART, T. (1981) Play and theatre *SCYPT Journal* 7
MEDWAY, P. (1980) *Finding A Language* (Writers and Readers)
MOFFETT, J. (1968) *Teaching the Universe of Discourse* (Boston: Houghton Mifflin)
WAGNER, B. J. (1976) *Drama as a Learning Medium* (Hutchinson)

JONOTHAN NEELANDS

Foreword

First, I want to commend the title of this book, for it describes exactly its purpose and its value: *Making Sense of Drama*. Jon Neelands and I have talked frequently over the last couple of years about drama, and he has often shown me bits of writing he has been working on – a number of which eventually formed part of this book. So I have seen him working hard to make sense of drama – for himself and for the teachers he works with. Initially this book was conceived as an in-service handbook for Northamptonshire teachers. Now it has a wider audience, and I think it should prove immensely helpful to many teachers.

In a sense there is nothing new in this book, for what Jon has tried to do is to synthesize, consolidate, and elucidate in a commonsense manner the understandings about drama in education which have been developed in recent years and make them accessible to a wider educational audience. However, I think that in mapping out the overall terrain he has helped us to see more clearly the relationship between some of the features, and he has cast some new and interesting light on particular areas. I for one found that what he had to say about the learning contract in drama clarified a number of things for me.

I think Jon's background has helped him considerably in his task: a background partly in English teaching and an involvement in classroom research in English has enabled him to look at the theory and practice of drama with habits of mind acquired outside the world of drama in education.

Close analysis of classroom processes and attempts to explain them in commonsense language are probably more familiar in the sphere of English teaching than in that of drama. His familiarity with this work has helped Jon to look closely at drama practice and to examine and tease out many of its common assumptions and terms of reference rather than simply accept them.

Every human activity (drama in education included) has an inevitable tendency to develop its own language and I have known many teachers who are baffled by 'dramajargon'. Jon's attempt to elucidate current drama thinking is therefore a very valuable service, for the whole point of drama as a way of teaching/learning is that *any* teacher can use it – it is a basically simple process (though that doesn't mean an easy one) available to serve a wide range of teaching/learning purposes. Obviously Jon will have succeeded in elucidating some areas better than others, and will not have wholly escaped the clutches of the dramajargon beast.
not have wholly escaped the clutches of the dramajargon beast.

As Jon himself stresses it is a book written 'on the move' – a snapshot of the sense he made of drama at the time of writing and of the best way he could then find of explaining it. By the time it is published obviously he will have moved on. This is so with any book and any writer. My reason for stressing it here is that this particular book is very definitely conceived as a 'provisional statement' – and you the reader will get most from it if you recognize that.

I see it as a book to be *used* rather than read, to be questioned rather than listened to. Once familiar with the general layout of the book, you can go at any time to a particular section and 'mine it' as your current needs and interest require. Approach it in a questioning spirit with your own purposes and needs clearly in mind. Twice in the book, in different ways, Jon explicitly invites the reader to adopt an active stance in relation to the material – he asks you to place yourself in an interrogative, active relationship to the ideas he is offering you. Do accept his invitation as this is the way the book should be read.

KEN BYRON

chapter 1
Introduction

This book is aimed principally at teachers working with children in the middle years of schooling although it is, perhaps, general enough to be a resource for infant and upper secondary teachers as well.

I hope that it will be read as a helpful guide rather than as prescriptive guidelines. It is not intended to be a definitive statement of good practice; nor is it comprehensive enough to cover every aspect of dramatic activity. It tends instead to deal with those aspects that teachers most ask for help with, and to skate over those aspects that are well dealt with in other publications.

The most noticeable omission is an account of how provision for drama needs to change as a child develops through the school years. There are, of course, numerous references to working with different ages, but there is not, for example, a detailed examination of what sort of drama best suits an eight-year-old's learning needs and energies as opposed to a 13-year-old's. My feeling is that it will take us a long time to gather enough accounts of classroom practice across the age-range to be able to make such detailed developmental observations. In the meantime, I hope this book will fill a gap for those teachers who are keen to develop their own drama practice.

So as a reader you will need to remember that the book is deliberately unspecific about the enormous differences within just the eight to 14 range. You may not be able to use some of the material as it is presented here with your class; it may look, or sound, too young or too old for them. You will need to use your existing experience to select from and modify what is offered so that it fits you and your class more exactly.

Ideally, you should start at the beginning and read through the entire book - but that might not suit your purpose for one of the following reasons:

1   It is a highly condensed account of a process that can operate at a number of levels - from the superficial level of games through to the deepest levels of whole-group role-play. You may therefore want to take your time getting through the book so that you can digest it in manageable 'chunks'.

2   You may not be interested in some of the directions taken in the book. You may just want the lesson plans in Chapter 10 or the descriptions of different ways of working in Chapter 6.

3   You may be interested in looking at drama from a particular viewpoint and making that your focus – for instance, you may want to concentrate on drama as 'theatre form' (Chapter 7) or on drama as a specialized form of classroom negotiation (Chapter 3).

In order to try and cater for these different purposes, it has been necessary to create overlaps, with the same material recurring in several different chapters; without this repetition the individual sections would be difficult to follow. In some cases, this repetition has a further purpose; it may be important to return to an idea that has already been touched upon in order to look at it from a different angle. Role, for instance, is looked at as a form of negotiation in Chapter 5; as part of the planning process in Chapter 9; as a concept in 'Theatre form'. So your sense of *déja vu* is justified!

The ordering of the chapters is intended to lead the reader from looking at drama as an extension of conventional classroom practice towards dealing with the more complex interrelationships between theatre form and classroom drama. Rather than adding additional information, the later chapters try instead to move to deeper levels of the drama experience.

A View of Learning

The book is based upon a theory of knowledge and learning that firmly recognizes the child's own resources for learning as valid and useful tools for classroom use. Children are not seen as passive recipients but as active meaning-makers who have already made considerable learning progress in their immediate environment before they ever come into classrooms. This early learning has not been characterized by the acquisition of objective theories about the world, but by sensual and practical involvement with it. Children show us, before they come to school and also later on when they tackle learning tasks out of school, that they learn best by making and doing. We can also see that children, habitually, use their existing experience as a means of making sense of new experience/information, and that if we give them the opportunity to build these bridges between what they already know and the new learning presented by school, we are also giving them *status* as learners and enabling them to refine their own ways of learning; we help them to learn how to learn.

I'm drawing attention to children's unique ways of seeing themselves and the world around them and the way those perceptions develop in response to the changing worlds of home and school... their way of perceiving is unique (roughly between the ages of eight and thirteen) in its buoyant openness and directness. Most adults' ability to see straight to the heart of something is filmed over with years of routine, convention and unself-critical habit, whereas many children possess a curiosity and a sense of wonder that gives rise to refreshingly honest insights. (Jackson)

There is also within this view of learning an acceptance that children work on experience, in order to discover its meanings, in a fundamentally different way from some adults.

In order to make what we call 'knowledge' out of experience we, *as teachers*, order and define it through various *disciplines* of thought which emerge in schools as subject areas. We interpret the world differently according to whether we view it with the eyes of a scientist, or a historian, or an environmentalist, or an artist.

For children, the world is still a new phenomenon. They have less actual experience than us. They still rely upon their imaginings and data processed through their senses rather than through their intellects as means of acting on and understanding new information and experience.

What I am suggesting is that in order to survive and understand in our environment, we have all developed ways of limiting and controlling our experience to the extent where we can put it into manageable forms that allow us to make sense of it. We reconstruct experience into forms of knowledge that we can understand, and that are familiar to us.

As teachers we tend to value and promote those forms of knowledge in which objectivity and the establishment of impersonal truth have a special learning value. In schools that foster a traditional curriculum superior status is often attached to those disciplines/forms of knowledge which clearly separate the scientific (in the broadest sense) from the personal and intuitive. The message that comes across is that learning through disciplines that value objectivity is more reliable, desirable and useful than learning through disciplines that combine cognition with personal, usually affective, responses.

In everyday life, of course, we do not order and define experiences through disciplines that separate us from our environment. We see ourselves at the centre looking out. We try to understand ourselves in relation to what goes on around us. In everyday life we value personal ways of knowing above impersonal 'truths'. Whatever our vocation and educational background, we do not live and experience at street-level as physicists, historians, sociologists or environmental scientists; our everyday experience is at a vernacular level, not a scientific one. The importance of this distinction is that *whereas children need to be initiated into school-forms of knowledge, they already possess, as a*

3

result of out-of-school learning, a degree of mastery in vernacular forms of knowledge. If schools reject the personal and vernacular in total favour of the impersonal and objective, they run the risk of ditching the children's own valuable learning resources and of making it impossible for many children ever to bridge the familiar with the unfamiliar; the reference points for learning of any kind will be destroyed.

The Bullock Report's view was:

> It is a confusion of everyday thought that we tend to regard 'knowledge' as something that exists independently of someone who knows. 'What is known' must in fact be brought to life afresh within every 'knower' by his own efforts . . . in order to accept what is offered when we are told something, we have to have somewhere to put it; and having somewhere to put it means that the framework of past knowledge and experience into which it must fit is adequate as a means of interpreting and apprehending it. (DES, 1975, para 4.9)

If we agree with this view then it makes sense for us, as teachers, to raise the status in our classrooms of the vernacular experience and ways of knowing that children bring with them into schools. By so doing, we are legitimizing the child's own efforts to make sense of new information by working on it with familiar tools and by fitting it into her pattern of previous and familiar experience. Furthermore, we avoid creating a confusing, and artificial, separation between school ways of knowing (subject disciplines) and street ways of knowing (vernacular forms); between the scientific and the personal and intuitive.

The assumption that underpins this viewpoint on learning in schools is that there must be a clear focus on *process* in the classroom (in contrast to views of learning that are child-centred or content-centred *per se*).

A process-centred education provides an authentic mirroring of 'real-life' learning where new problems are synthesized through structures and methods formulated to enable effective discovery – the detective hunting for clues, the scientist testing her hypothesis through research. The purpose of process-centred learning is to enable children to discover, *for themselves*, new meanings – not to inculcate tired, well-worn meanings as is the case in content-centred education.

Throughout this book there is a twin emphasis upon the vernacular processes of *story* (narrative) and *play* (game), the assumption being that these are conventional ways of knowing for children. As Barbara Hardy says of story: 'My argument is that narrative, like lyric or dance, is not to be regarded as an aesthetic invention used by artists . . . but as a *primary act of mind* transferred to art from life . . . in order to live we make up stories about ourselves and others, about the personal as well as the social past and future.'

Although the important, and distinctive, differences between story

Everyday knowledge and cultural resources*

1 Proverbs
2 Rhymes
3 Riddles
4 Games
5 Laws
6 Rules
7 Punishments
8 Sayings
9 Stories
  a stories I've been told
  b stories my parents know
  c stories my grandparents know
10 Happenings and events in the history of our people
  a recent in my life
  b in my parents' lives
  c in my grandparents' lives
11 Jokes
12 Special Days - e.g. 'What we do on ... day'
13 Songs
14 Places we go
  a private, secret
  b public and social
  c 'hanging-about' places
15 Celebrations and feasts
16 Foods - favourite dishes and recipes
17 'The way we do it' - e.g. The garden, Dressing, Hair, Decorating our rooms.
18 Hobbies, pastimes, pursuits, 'activities', 'crazes'
19 Music
20 Sports
  a participatory
  b spectator
21 Kinds of work done by our people
  a me
  b parents
  c grandparents
  d brothers and sisters
  e interviewed people - e.g. workers in the news
  f housework - who does what? is this fair?
  g losing work/looking for work/ living without work
22 Courtship, marriage, weddings and alternatives

23 Holidays, favourite places
24 Outings
  a organized
  b unorganized
25 Slangs, dialects, in-group jargons and new words
26 Family sagas
27 Street spectacles
28 a superstitions and charms
  b oaths, secrets - e.g. about hidden, illicit deeds
29 Street cries, market traders, bus conductors, pub calls etc.
30 True or false: local legends or myths, historic and contemporary
31 'It's not fair!' - morals: who are the wrongdoers (cheats, conmen, cruel people)? who are the right-doers (friends in need)?
32 Heroes, heroines, anti-heroes, anti-heroines: local, showbiz, national, international, historic
33 Victims and scapegoats
  a you as a victim or scapegoat
  b you victimizing or scapegoating others
34 Loyalties: taking sides (brother v. brother, v. sister, mother v. father, girls v. boys), the gang, the football team, the 'nation', the community, styles (Rude Boys, Punk), trade union, school, political party, church, class, ethnic group
  Divided loyalties: between two cultures, where do I belong?
35 Battlegrounds
  a places - street, estate, playground, park
  b types - fights, campaigns, marches, petitions, strikes
36 Clubs and organizations
37 What do boys do (according to boys, girls)?
38 What do girls do (according to boys, girls)?
39 The future, real and imagined
40 Death - deaths I have known, seen, heard about; bereavement.
41 Will it always be like this?

*From Mike Rosen, *Becoming Our Own Experts*.

and play will be drawn out during the book, my assumption is that play, like story, is a primary act of mind transferred to art from *life*.

In considering this view of learning it might be useful for us to take notice of the work done by Mike Rosen who has compiled a list representing the everyday experience and forms of knowledge that all children possess in part, whatever their ability, background or ethnicity. I have reproduced the list in the hope that you will find it useful and illuminating not just for your drama work, but for the other areas of your teaching as well (see p. 5).

A View of Drama

The view of learning I have described has in turn shaped a view of drama that seeks to develop and extend children's existing cultural resources in ways that are both familiar and also stretching. This view of drama is developed through the book, but it may be briefly summarized as:

1   Drama should be unequivocally child-centred (i.e. it makes use of existing language, experience, motivations and interests); but at the same time learning through drama depends upon a form of teacher intervention which aims to bring new shapes and fresh ways of knowing to children's existing experience of play and other forms of interactive and imitative behaviour. (Educational drama is seen as a personal and cultural *development* of this experience.)

2   Drama (in the educational context) is not as concerned with the transmission of theatre-skills as it is with the construction of imagined experience. Imagined experience (controlled by the conventions of game and theatre) is seen as being a particularly efficient context for children to try out and experiment with new ideas, concepts, values, roles and language in action (i.e. in the situational context in which they would naturally occur). Drama is to do with the child experiencing rather than with the child performing.

3   Drama is practical, immediate and engages the emotions as well as the intellect (it seeks to *bond* the personal and intuitive with the scientific). Drama brings a dimension of ACTION to classroom learning through the imagined use of TIME – SPACE – PEOPLE.

4   Drama is a social (interactive) way of creating and interpreting human meanings through imagined action and language that simulates and corresponds to real-life actions and language (the imagined experience should possess a real-life quality for the participants).

5   Drama is seen as an active process which is useful to learners if it is *appropriately introduced*. It is not seen as a subject or as a distinct curriculum area (we will not be considering theatre arts). It is not quantifiable or academic, nor is it seen as having specifiable inputs and

outputs. It is seen instead as *a classroom resource* that should be available to every learner and teacher to make use of in much the same way as art and craft materials are available, i.e. as and when required.

6 Drama is not dependent on specialists or hall space (although drama is unquestionably developed by access to both); it is intended for *all* teachers working in whatever space is available to them.

7 The kind of drama that is emphasized is at a point on a continuum that has its genesis in child-play and its furthest cultural and personal development in the art-form of theatre (see Chapter 7). In other words, the teacher is attempting to match the child's existing experience of play to the less familiar forms of theatre in order to focus and deepen the child's learning experience.

References

DES (1975) *A Language for Life* (The Bullock Report) (HMSO)
HARDY, B. (1977) in M. Meek (ed.) *The Cool Web* (Bodley Head)
JACKSON, D. (1982) *Continuity in Secondary English* (Methuen)
ROSEN, M. (1982) in *Becoming Our Own Experts* (English Centre)

chapter 2
Beowulf – A Sample Lesson

In order to place this book within a context of actual practice, this chapter consists of a sequence of work represented through transcript and description. The session is not analysed in any way nor is it edited; the transcript is a record of everything that was said (and some of what was done) during an actual lesson. I felt that it might be useful to have a lesson presented in this way for several reasons:

1 You might find it interesting at this stage in the book to have an uninterrupted account of a lesson so that you have some idea of how the view of learning and view of drama outlined in the Introduction translate into classroom practice.

2 It is too soon at this stage in the book to provide an analysis of what is going on beneath the surface of the lesson – it might well confuse rather than clarify. The remainder of the book deals with the 'how and why' behind the work represented here – I hope questions that occur to you as you read through the transcript may be answered later. I would strongly recommend you to use the transcript to frame your own list of questions about drama as they occur, and to keep a list of those questions at your side as you move on. You may find satisfactory answers later on, or you may be left with questions that will require *you* to research *your* own practice in order to come to satisfactory answers.

3 Hopefully the example given will serve as a useful resource in a variety of ways. You might use it as material for looking at the *role of the teacher* in drama; for looking at varieties of *language use*; for looking at the nature of *questions* in drama; for looking at *planning* and *evaluation*; as a model for a lesson of your own; as a focus for an in-service session – or simply as a straightforward illustration of drama in practice.

So I hope for these reasons that you do not become frustrated by the absence of detailed commentary during the transcript and that you accept that its purpose is *not* to provide a lesson-plan or scheme of work that could be followed by another group.

Why Choose this Lesson?

The Beowulf lesson has not been chosen to serve as an exemplar. It is a lesson that is interesting in some ways, but as in all of the lessons that we teach there are elements that work well and elements that go astray. There are many ways of using drama, and no single sequence of work can be raised up as a model for *all* drama work. Within the lesson described here are a number of strategies, ideas and principles at work that underpin much of the thinking in this book; but the lesson itself could have been organized in a variety of different ways – its construction is not as significant as its *intentions*.

The organizing principle of any drama work should not be what other teachers and their groups have done but instead WHAT'S POSSIBLE? Of course talking with other teachers and observing their work are invaluable ways of expanding and enriching our ideas about what is possible, but in the end the considerations must be:

What's possible for me?
With this group?
In this space?
In the time I have available?

In the Beowulf lesson I had possibilities that would ordinarily be denied to most classroom teachers. (In fact you may well feel that I only scratched at the surface of the possibilities available to me!)

I was working as an advisory teacher. (I had no real knowledge of the group as individuals.)
I was working with only seventeen children. (The construction would have been very different with a larger group.)
I was working in a very small space. (As a result there is little physical action – it's a static, chair-bound session.)
I was able to control the length of the session. (I was not bound by bells, breaks or timetables.)
I am relatively experienced in using drama. (I have had the opportunity to develop this experience; I might have handled the King–Beowulf conflict differently with less experience.)

These are the circumstances that defined for me 'What's possible?' and they should be borne in mind when you read the lesson. These circumstances also affected the choice of the Beowulf session as an illustration in the following way:

The lesson is very static in terms of action; it is therefore possible to give a comprehensive picture of the lesson through transcript. Some lessons hang on the actions, or pauses, or symbolic gestures, or facial

9

expressions. Such lessons would be very difficult to describe in writing.

The lesson took place in a classroom and is a useful illustration of what's possible if no other space is available. How many of us work in carpeted drama studios? The teacher remains in control, acting as chairperson for all that is said, i.e. it's a fairly safe structure. (In fact, he remains too much in control!) The lesson was not an easy one for the teacher to maintain and as a result it's perhaps more interesting than a smooth and slick lesson might have been. (Many of the problems stem from the conflict with Beowulf – a girl who totally amazed her teacher with her uncharacteristic defiance. *But* this conflict was also the mainspring of the lesson.)

Because it wasn't an easy lesson the teacher had to employ a wide range of strategies in his negotiations with the group. If I list the strategies I consider to be at work in the lesson, it might be useful for *you* to tie them into the transcript as and when you recognize them.

1   Using teacher-in-role to initiate the drama; using a leader-authority role (see pp. 47, 51).

2   A variety of forms of questioning (see pp. 36*ff.*).

3   Planning both in and out of role (see pp. 43–46, 46–57).

4   A different but productive teacher-learner relationship (see pp. 24–32, 36, 46).

5   Whole-group interaction (see pp. 50, 63).

6   Use of space and time (see pp. 70–71, 77).

7   Coping with responses (see pp. 40*ff.*).

8   Spontaneous development of the drama (see pp. 31, 49–51).

9   Teacher's use of language (see p. 33).

10   Ritual (see pp. 67, 80).

11   Using a variety of ways of working (see p. 58).

12   Using and developing children's existing experience – both actual and from story (see pp. 2, 5, 6, 25, 26, 45, 82).

The lesson represents one teacher's handling of a theme and his attempts to draw a group into a productive relationship with it. It might be useful for you to consider your own ways into the material: How could the children have been moved into action more quickly? How could the teacher have used the ideas offered by the children more effectively? What other ways could the teacher have found to involve more of the group?

Preliminary Work on Beowulf

The Setting

Brixworth Primary School: 17 mixed nine- and ten-year-olds; one half-day (2½ hour) session; a self-contained classroom.

The thinking for the lesson came from a personal enthusiasm for Kevin Crossley-Holland's latest adaptation of *Beowulf*, illustrated by Charles Keeping and published by the Oxford University Press. I was impressed by the way the author had managed to make the text more manageable, and more appealing, for younger readers. In doing so he has retained the wonderful aural colour and rich, physical imagery of the verse-story. The text is sensuously matched by Charles Keeping's barbarous and harsh drawings.

I was also interested by the 'old chestnut' reputation that *Beowulf* has amongst drama teachers. It has appeal as a dramatic context for the same reasons, I suspect, as those which made it so popular a spoken story in older times. (For an alternative account of *Beowulf* as drama see O'Neill and Lambert.) There is much to respond to in this epic legend of honour, courage, monsters, duty and sacrifice.

The group had previously looked at *Elidor* by Alan Garner in a variety of ways, including drama, and I thought that drama might again provide a useful tool for them to use in order to penetrate the text more fully and closely.

The Session

In our first meeting we had read slowly the first fourteen pages of the text and stopped at the point where Beowulf and his band settle down in Heorot to wait for Grendel.

I purposefully chose this point because I wanted to work with the *children's* imaginings of what Grendel *might* be like. I wanted to stop before Grendel was defined by the storyteller; this would give the group the chance to consider facing a monster of their own making.

In our reading of the first part of the story I had asked the group to register any signs given in the text as to the nature of Beowulf's world – the customs, the atmosphere, the surroundings. After we had discussed their findings I asked the group to split into fours and to work together on producing a group image of Grendel using white and black charcoal. At this point I hadn't shown them any of Charles Keeping's drawings because I felt they might inhibit original interpretations.

When the group finished their drawings we sat together and looked at each in turn. We then began to talk about the tapestries described in the book. Someone remembered that some of those represented monsters also and we talked about what the other tapestries might have represented – kings, heroic deeds, battles, great adventures. I asked them to return to their small groups and to work on preparing tableaux representing the 'golden-eyed tapestries winking out of the gloom'.

When they were ready to show their work we assembled as a large group and I addressed them as the curator of a museum. I explained that we were fortunate enough to have been given a stone casket which had been unearthed near Brixworth Church (a Saxon church). The casket contained tapestries from the time of the Viking raids. I welcomed the group as historians, archeologists and art-historians and asked them for help in deciphering the tapestries and in giving the museum some idea of the significance of each picture – 'What does it tell us about the people who treasured it?'

Each group in turn then showed us their tableau and the experts discussed it as if they were looking at a real tapestry. When we finished, the group asked to take on the roles in the story. They were keen to try out being the Geats and to face their own fearsome Grendels! We arranged the chairs so that they were in an open circle (see Fig. 1, below). The following is a transcript of what went on during that role-play.

Fig. 1   Classroom layout during Beowulf transcript

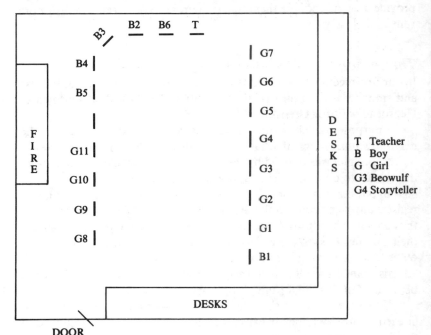

The Transcript

T Teacher; B Boy; G Girl; Be Beowulf; S Storyteller; C Chorus – several voices more or less simultaneously. Unless otherwise stated, everyone remains seated in the positions indicated in Figure 1.

T	Where is this happening – this first part of the story?
B2	In England?
T	In what sort of place?
G10	In a big hall.
T	A big hall – how would you imagine that hall?
B1	Heavy wooden tables, big long ones.
G4	And glass chandeliers.
B4	Enormous fireplaces.
T	Anything else? . . . would it be a tall, high place do you think?
C	Yes.
T	And would it be all clear and clean?
C	No.
T	How would it be?
B1	Beer mugs everywhere.
B4	Bits.
T	Bits?
B4	Bits of food.
T	Yes . . . so we're in the hall of the Geats. How would we be dressed?
G8	Long robes.
B4	Cloaks and big belts with great metal buckles.
G10	Sandals.
T	Sort of sandals yeah – what about our hair, would it be wonderfully clean and . . . ?
C	No.
G4	Dirty.
T	What, sort of long and lankish (gestures) – a bit like mine today?

(Nods)

T	And would we be all smooth-faced?
C	No – beards.
T	Sort of rough beards – so we're pretty tough are we?
C	Yeah.
T	How do we think of ourselves then, us Geats?
G8	We think we're the greatest.
C	Yeah.
T	Yes, we're pretty tough eh? We've fought some good battles in our time hmm?

C   Yeah.

T   Nobody dares quarrel with the Geats.

C   No.

T   Right – so I'm going to be Hygelac, King of the Geats – now there are two other roles that we want to use in this opening. The first role is a very difficult one, it's the role of the story-teller. Who thinks they will be able to take the role of the storyteller? (*B1, 3, 4, 5, G2, 1, 3, 4, 8 raise hands.*) You do (*indicates G4*) OK. And the other difficult role is . . . who thinks they will be able to take the role of Beowulf?(*B1, 2, 3, 4, 5, G8, 3, 1 raise hands.*) Right! (*indicates G3*). So story-teller would you like to come over and put this on? (*G4 moves to centre. T helps her to put on a 'Saxon' cloak.*)

G2   She looks like Little Red Riding Hood. (*laughs*)

T   (*To G4*) Would you like to go over there and enter from there? (*indicates doorway*) But give us a chance to settle down. Just wait a while, while we find out what it is like to be Geats. (*G4 looks unsure.*) I'll give you a signal, OK?

G4   Yeah.

T   Ah, well, so Geats, as we're sitting here drinking and eating, what stories does anyone have to tell us? What adventures has anyone had? Anybody done anything daring and exciting recently?

B1   Only thing that's exciting, that's what's happened is . . . there've been some good scraps.

T   You have had some good fights then, recently?

B1   Yeah.

T   Who've they been against then?

B1   Galactica.

T   Ah, he's been causing trouble again then has he?

(*B1 nods*)

T   And did you sort him out?

B1   Just about, yeah.

T   Good, Anybody else? (*waits*) Any other adventures? (*waits*) Ah, times are quiet in Hygelac's Court. Nothing ever happens. What about you Beowulf, you're always boasting of your bravery.

Be   Too quiet for me.

T   Too quiet, huh, perhaps the young lad wants a taste of adventure, eh!

C   Yeah.

T   You'll soon learn there's more to life than fighting . . . there's drinking to be done, too! Anyway, it's a pity those storytellers don't come round anymore – stories to stir your blood. (*gestures G3*)

(*Storyteller 'knocks'*)
- G10 There's someone at the door.
- S I come to tell you a story!
- T You've come to tell us a story!

(*Clapping*)
- T We're pretty fierce people you know. I hope you have a story that's suitable.
- S I come to tell you a story about a great big dragon.
- T That sounds like the kind of stuff we like, eh?
- C Yes, yes.
- T Go on then Storyteller, you tell us!
- S Beowulf came to find this dragon. (*Stops*)
- T Beowulf? Same name as my son here. What sort of dragon was this?
- S I can't explain it was so terrible (*swirls her cloak and turns*) and everyone that came to fight it got killed.

(*Reaction of fear*)
- T Where does this dragon live?
- S In a hall, a great hall.
- T And where is this hall?
- S Heorot.
- T In Heorot.

(*Gasps*)
- S In the land of the Danes. It comes every midnight.
- T Midnight? Why don't the Danes sort it out, they're tough?
- S Beowulf (*turns and points with outstretched arm*) you have a go.
- Be (*Jumps up*) Alright, I will. I'll get my men and I'll go. (*walks off, turns*) Come on!
- T Wait a minute, wait a minute. Beowulf sit you down. (*Beowulf returns to seat.*) Here Stranger have a seat with us. (*Storyteller sits.*) Now this monster he speaks of, this Grendel. He says it frightens the Danes.
- Be We're, we're stronger than them.
- T Well we may be now, but it's not always been that way. Remember we used to have to pay tribute to the Danes?
- C Yeah, yes.
- T We used to have to pay the Danes money or else they would invade our villages. Why should we help them?
- B2 We don't even know it there is a monster.
- T No . . . what do you say?
- B4 I think we could leave it there. Teach them a lesson.

15

C   Yeah.

Be (*Stands*) I don't care. I'm going.

T   For what purpose Beowulf?

Be I want to kill it. (*stamps foot*)

T   Do you think he's the kind of . . . will the Danes let him fight the dragon?

Be I'll prove it.

T   You've got a wild tongue in your head – take a seat.

Be No.

T   Beowulf, you don't stand in my court.

Be I want to take my men.

T   Listen to those who are older and wiser than you – talk this through first.

(*Beowulf sits*)

B1 She won't even get in the waters.

T   That's right. Do you think the Danes will even let you land?

G11 I think he should go.

T   Why's that?

G11 Well, he could have a try.

Be (*Stands*) I don't care if I get killed. At least I will have tried. I want my men. And I want to go.

T   Why do you think you're going to be any better than the Danes who've tried to fight?

G10 Yes.

B4 Yes.

Be When they came to us . . . that was ages ago.

T   And what do you think has happened since then?

Be I don't know. They could have got weaker. They could have got stronger. I don't know.

T   Well, has anyone else heard? Have the Danes got weaker?

B3 Stronger.

C   Yes, stronger.

Be They're probably just drunken idiots.

B5 Go and tell that to their Chief.

C   Yes.

T   Anyway, we had to pay the Danes. If we're sending people to help, we should get paid. What do we want from them?

B1 Food.

G4 Food.

G9 Possessions.

Be Nothing.

(*Long pause*)

T   Nothing?

Be	I'm going whether you want me to or not.
T	Well, wait a minute. We don't know whether anybody is going to go with you.
Be	I'm taking them. I'll have you (*G2*), you (*G4*), you (*G5*).
T	Wait a minute Beowulf. You're too anxious. These things need careful preparation. Ships need to be armed – and food put on board. You need to pick the right people. It's no good picking people who will be no use in such a struggle.
B3	Yeah.
G9	Yeah.
T	Take a seat. (*Beowulf sits.*) First, Beowulf, you tell us what equips you for this task. What have you done in the past?
Be	I don't know. I just want to try. It could be my first and help me to do others.
T	Olag (*gestures towards B1*) you had the task of training Beowulf in combat, how has he done with his training?
B1	(*Pauses, rubs his chin.*) He's done quite good (*pause*) I'm not sure if he can go.
T	Now Olag. Beowulf says he is ready for his first task, his first mission – what is your opinion?
B1	(*Pause*) I don't know.
T	What sort of people should we send with him?
B1	Good strong ones.
T	Experienced warriors?
B1	Yeah.
Be	I want to pick my own.
T	You will decide but Olag and the rest of us will guide you in this choice.
B1	I reckon he can go.
T	And he will bring honour back to this hall?
B1	Yeah. Hopefully yeah.
T	And will you go along to protect him?
B1	Yeah.

. . . . .

T	Now who else amongst you has performed tasks that might be useful to us?
Be	Father!
T	Wait a minute, let him speak. (*points to B4*)
B4	Well, the villagers have attacked this place dozens of times. Me and my two fellows here (*puts his hands on the shoulders of B3 and B5*) we've just been throwing boulders about that big (*gestures*) at them. (*B3 and B5 nod*)
B2	Morag.

B3   Yeah.

B5   And the dragon of Troy.

B2   Yeah.

T   Ah, so you have experience in dealing with monsters.

B2,3,4,5   Yeah.

T   And how did you trap this monster?

B3   We made an old Indian trap (*gestures*) and when it was down there we chucked our spears down onto it.

Be   I don't want those three, they're spiteful. (*Stands*)

T   What do you mean spiteful?

Be   (*Stands*) They are always jeering at me. I want him (*G1*), him (*G6*), him (*G7*).

T   Beowulf, you are not yet King. Take your seat. (*Pause, then Beowulf sits.*) You will be guided by your father in this matter. These (*indicates B3, 4, 5*) are three experienced warriors. Now who else?

G8   Us four (*gestures towards G9, 10, 11*) have fought Romans. Many of them.

T   Yes, so you think you are equipped to fight?

G8   Sure we are.

T   Are there any of you who have something to prove, who may wish to risk your lives in this adventure? Any of you who feel there is something to prove?

(*Pause*)

T   Yes.

G10   To prove there is a monster.

T   To prove it's not just a story.

G10   Yes.

G8   So that we can kill it.

B1   Prove who's boss.

B2   We don't even know how big it is yet.

T   We don't even know how big it is.

B1   How do we get into the waters first?

T   We will go by ship. We will prepare a large ship.

Be   (*Stands*) We? I want to go by myself.

T   You will have the lives of many others to consider. You must control your recklessness. Many of those that leave this hall will not come back – and we need to know their blood will bring honour back to this hall; not be lost in a foolhardy adventure.

Be   Yes, father.

T   And Olag. He's not too big for a clip . . . What preparations should these warriors make?

B4 We could make deadly spears.

B2 Fireballs.

T Sorry?

B2 Fireballs.

T Yes, we could make some tarred fireballs.

Be I will take a few of everything. We don't know what he's like. So we might need anything.

T Wise words Beowulf. It's best to be well prepared. Yes?

G4 Poisoned food.

T Poisoned food? What might poisoned food be used for do you think?

G4 Well it might like to eat . . . like some chicken and poison it and leave it for the monster.

T Right. Yes. OK.

B1 We'll have to get some wild berries first for p__ pro__ p__ (*struggles for word*) provisions.

T Yes, and how will we need to prepare ourselves in our heads and in our hearts . . . how will we need to prepare ourselves?

B1 (*Without mockery*) I've got some helmets in the back yard.

T Yes?

B4 Shields.

B3 We'll need the best shields.

G6 And the thickest armour we can get.

T Yes, any other suggestions?

G2 Train more men.

Be But father, it will take too long. I want to go now.

T Well, be patient. Yes?

G8 We'll need fireproof armour just in case this Grendel, as the stranger calls it, breathes fire.

T That is very wise.

Be If we fight with anything. I'll fight with my bare hands as well. Bare fight.

T Brave words Beowulf. Brave words. Let's see how you speak when you face the monster.

B6 We will need mirror shields. Just in case its eyes can turn you into stone.

T That's right.

Be (*Stands*) I don't want too much stuff. It'll make the ship sink. I want to go my own way.

T Be advised Beowulf.

Be You advise me too much.

T Will someone speak to my son?

B4 If you get more stuff, you can kill it easier. The ship won't

     sink, because we can make more. Then the ships. The ships
     can go faster if we make more.
T   Yes.
G2   And he doesn't realize how big the monster is.
T   Olag, perhaps you should remind her what happened the last
     time we went unprepared to the land of the Danes.
B1   Yes. We were beaten. I still feel the shame.
Be   You think, you think you know everything.
T   Old heads are wiser than young heads Beowulf and you need
     to rem . . .

Beowulf interrupts
Be   Young spirits are stronger than old spirits father.
T   Young spirits may well be stronger. But you need the
     experience of our years. Our bodies carry the scars of many
     battles.
B3   If you don't want to listen to us let the Grendel monster kill
     you.
B1   Stranger, how big is this Grendel?
S   I've heard it's two . . . well, he's so big it's difficult. He's
     bigger than this (*points to roof*) – it's two times bigger than
     this.

(*Gasps, sighs*)
B4   When we killed a dragon that size it took us four hundred
     men, not thirty.
T   That's true.
G8   When are we going to see this dragon, as you call it?
S   In the Danes' hall at 12 o'clock.
B2   But what if we fall asleep?
Be   I won't fall asleep that's for sure.
G9   Stranger, how many heads has this monster got?
S   Three.
T   Three. So it will see in every direction.
S   And nine eyes.
G1   I will cut off one of its legs.
T   Has anyone else questions about Grendel?
G2   How tough is its skin?
S   Well, it's as thick as these walls.

(*Gasps*)
T   Well, swords and poisoned spears will be no good will they?
B2   How fast is it?
S   90 m.p.h.

(*Laughter from several*)
T   Remember, he is only a storyteller.

C   Yes.

T   As fast as a fast dog?

S   Much faster . . . how are we going to trap it then?

B4   We could use nets. So it would run into them.

B6   But if it runs so fast, it could break the nets.

G4   When it comes into the hall, someone could push the table against the door. Then we could surround it and kill it.

B2   Well, if you had nets this monster, if it is true, could just pull them apart.

T   Yes, what about the suggestion we've just had over there? Yes?

G10   If it turns around its tail will kill all of us.

S   And he's ninety-nine stone.

(Gasps)

B4   He'll break the table.

T   So has anyone else any suggestions? The Danes must have had ideas that haven't worked, so we need to go with a good plan. Olag, yes?

B1   If we get a big log and trip it over, then we can get a big boulder and smash it on its head.

G6   It might run straight through it.

B3   Go for its legs.

G2   Storyteller, does it eat actual human beings?

S   Pardon?

G2   Does he eat actual people?

S   Yes.

(Gasps)

G8   We should heat up iron and push it in his eyes.

C   Yes, yeah. *(Some clap)*

T   That idea finds favour with you does it?

C   Yes!

The planning continued for another ten minutes, then I asked the warriors to return home to prepare themselves. In pairs, they improvised their farewells, with an emphasis upon reassuring and explaining. The partners who were being left behind reported back about their feelings and anxieties at that moment – was it fair to them for their partners to go on such an adventure?

The group again took on the roles of warriors and assembled on the dock, in the early morning, ready to board ship.

T   Stand in a line, warriors. (*They assemble carrying spears and bundles.*) Four in a rank! Space out so that I can inspect you.

Now the other Geats are all around you watching. So stand and show them you are ready for this mission.

(*Teacher inspects the warriors, slowly. There is silence. Voices are very quiet. The conversation is private.*)

T   Are you prepared, Storyteller?
S   Yes. (*T moves on.*)
T   And you, are you prepared?
G2 Yes.
T   And have you brought anything special with you?
G2 Yes, my axe. (*T moves on.*)
T   Are you going to be warm enough?
G1 Yes.
T   Right. (*Moves on.*)
T   And you, you're young to be on this mission. Young to die. Have you thought about that?
G4 Yes.
T   And why are you so keen?
G4 To help get rid of the monster.
T   And have you brought anything special with you?
G4 Yes, a large spear my grandad gave me.
T   And have you said your farewells to your father and mother?
G4 Yes.

(*T carries on talking with every child.*)

T   Well Geats, you'll be boarding and leaving soon, taking the honour of the Geats with you. Now some of you have not been before. You may not know that we always speak the great oath of the Geats before we go. Perhaps some of the more experienced, of the oath ... who can remind us? ... perhaps you remember parts of it only? ... it's a long time since we set out like this ... Yes?
B2 A part of it is, we will bring back the oaths of the giant creatures.
T   We will bring back the oaths of the giant creatures – can anyone else remember?
B3 We shall trap them.
T   We shall trap them – and can anyone remember the parts that are to do with honour and courage that we are looking for?
G10 And wisdom.
T   And wisdom. What is the one motto we have, the motto we always say?
B2 Go proudly.
G8 Never boast.

T   Go proudly, never boast.

B1 All for one, one for all.

T   Yes. Go proudly, never boast. All for one. One for all.

C   Yes.

T   Let us hear you say it - and let's see you raise your weapons and shake them as we speak. GO PROUDLY NEVER BOAST.

All (*Raising weapons*) GO PROUDLY NEVER BOAST.

T   ALL FOR ONE, ONE FOR ALL.

All ALL FOR ONE, ONE FOR ALL.

T   Good luck, warriors!

Session ends.

References

CROSSLEY-HOLLAND, K. (1982) *Beowulf* (Oxford University Press)

GARNER, A. (1965) *Elidor* (Collins)

O'NEILL, C. and LAMBERT, A. (1982) *Drama Structures* (Hutchinson)

chapter 3
The Teacher-Learner Partnership in Drama

Drama is both a way of learning and a method of teaching, and we should be clear about both sides of that relationship. Drama makes its own kind of demands on both learners and teachers, and you and your group need to be prepared to adapt certain kinds of strategies to meet those demands.

It's important, and reassuring, to realize that the key strategies in drama are probably familiar to you and your group anyway, particularly those strategies that are concerned with establishing an appropriate relationship and climate for learning. It's likely that your classroom is probably already characterized by some of the teacher/learner attitudes described below.

Teacher Attitudes

1 You are willing to take *informed risks* in order to develop your own experience as a teacher, and you encourage children to do the same in order to broaden their horizons.

2 You allow your class some say in the organization of their own learning by encouraging self-assessment both for your group and for yourself through the use of journals (diaries, reading logs etc.) and by giving opportunities for pupil-to-pupil talk. Most significantly, you encourage children to make some of their own choices about materials for learning and ways of making sense of those materials.

3 You try not to appear as an omnipotent expert. You prefer to be seen as an *interested listener* rather than as teller. You are used to valuing *every* well-intentioned contribution that is made by your children, regardless of aptitude. Crucially, you help children to see their existing experience of the world as a valid and useful resource for further learning. You help children build bridges between what they already know and the new information presented by school-learning.

4 One of your aims is to help children discover their own voice and how to use it for their own purposes in a rich variety of situations. Your

priority is to give children the confidence to use language willingly by providing a sense of audience and a sense of purpose.

5   Your teaching is always within a context that offers the possibility of personally relevant *meanings for the child*; you don't offer a diet of disjointed exercises and drills. All learning in your classroom is applied to concrete, actual and purposeful situations.

Learner Attitudes

We should also remember the learning strategies that children bring with them to drama, even if they are inexperienced and unfamiliar with school drama.

1   Children are used to employing role-play as a strategy for making sense of other people's behaviours: we have seen them playing 'families', 'schools', 'war' etc., and we have noticed the disturbing accuracy of their portrayals of scolding mothers, angry schoolteachers and castaways in space.

2   We sense that children learn best by making and doing, and drama provides them with a physical and concrete resource for examining issues that might otherwise remain abstract and inaccessible. To illustrate this point, here is an anecdote about Robert Witkin's young son, who came back from school one lunchtime and remarked to his father that his mother was mad. His father asked him why and his son told him that as they were leaving for school in the morning, his mother had said to a neighbour, 'Nice day, isn't it?' This was madness because it had been pouring with rain at the time. Bob struggled to explain the concept of dramatic irony to his son and watched him walk off into the next room bewildered and confused. A few minutes later he returned. 'Come and see what I've done, Dad.' Bob went through, the room was a tip – furniture overturned, magazines and cushions scattered. His son looked up and said, 'Nice tidy room isn't it, Dad!'

A child needs to reconstruct abstract meaning into a form that she can deal with. When children reconstruct, whatever they make becomes their understanding.

3   Children are also used to the idea that games require rules and conditions if they are to work. Vygotsky made much of the importance of play and games to children in the sense that children *voluntarily* impose rules upon their own behaviour in order to make games work: 'If you want to play with us, you must keep to the rules'. So it is if you observe children playing: they take turns; when they are out, it's someone else's turn. Crucially, they accept that the outcome of a game is unknown. There wouldn't be much pleasure in playing football if the score was settled before the game started. There is a discipline that goes

on regardless of adult intervention. Drama is an extension of play activity; children are able to enjoy the same self-disciplining behaviour, and so is the teacher. Control should belong to the group. Rather than using the threat of sanctions to control behaviour, the teacher is able to use the lure of drama, and the need for rules and conventions to make it work, as an implicit control device.

4   We should be particularly aware of what children bring with them to drama from their experience of interpreting and constructing stories. In a sense, drama can be seen as a fictional activity that helps to illuminate/define real experience. Children are more familiar with making sense of the world through story than through factually-detached and textbook-bound approaches. David Jackson puts the point more succinctly:

> Stories, because of their unique power to shape absorbing scenes where people respond directly and immediately to one another and their ability to investigate, in highly specific ways, people's intentions, often make more spontaneous human sense than isolated factual statements or single units of meaning. And because of this, children seem to have a rare willingness to engage themselves in the complete satisfactions of listening to or making their own stories, thinking through anecdotes in the classroom, and wanting to understand other people's stories.

To that list I would add learning through dramatic activity; it's story of a significantly *different* kind to written or oral narratives, but it is a form of fiction none the less.

5   Children are also familiar with learning from each other and from adults other than teachers. Learning in school is often organized in such a way that learners are separated from each other, working individually and in competition with each other. Some children miss the informal collective learning that has characterized their out-of-school learning, and they are happiest in non-competitive social situations where there is a to and fro of ideas and suggestions made by a group intent on a mutual purpose. Drama fosters this kind of learning together.

The Demands of Working Together

If your intention is to set up opportunities for children to use drama by themselves, for themselves, without the teacher taking part (i.e. at a distance from you), then the attitudes outlined above are perhaps enough to make a start. You will only need some titles or exercises for them to work on. If you intend to work with your group *within* the drama – in other words if you are interested in taking a part yourself, shaping the play together as you go along – then you will need strategies to meet the demands made by that way of working. It's important to understand that unlike almost any other area of learning, spontaneous drama work cannot be imposed. You cannot set drama, or worse, coerce groups into it. A group has to move to a point where they are willing to work at a subjective level of involvement in open-ended pretending situations. Successful drama does not stem from silent obedience to a teacher's authority and status. (You can shout and scream that maths has to be done, or that spellings have to be learnt – but unless a child *willingly* enters the drama on her own terms, nothing will happen.) Drama requires forms of negotiation that allow for some bargaining between the teacher and the group, as to the nature and content of the work.

The Learning Contract for Drama

Many classrooms are already characterized by this bargaining climate in which learning is seen as a cooperative endeavour and in which the teacher takes a genuine interest in matching learning materials to the particular needs and interests of her pupils; but even so, a sharper form of negotiation may be needed by both partners in the learning *contract* for drama.

The contract itself may be implicit – it's already there and understood in the way you and your class relate to each other; or explicit – it's been discussed and negotiated openly with your class. *But it must be there.* It's no use going on to discuss the techniques and strategies of drama unless we are clear about the nature of that contract. It is a prerequisite of drama work. The contract can serve several purposes:

1   It establishes a partnership between teacher and group.
2   It defines the investment being made by all those involved: 'This is what I'm putting in and this is what I expect to take out'.
3   It reinforces the idea that drama makes its own kinds of demands on *both* teachers and pupils and that if any of those demands are avoided, the drama will lose its effect.
4   It demystifies drama both as a learning process and as an art-form (theatre): 'The teacher is not playing tricks with us'.
5   It provides a reference point for dealing with problems that may arise later: 'Which of the terms of the contract did we fall down over?'
6   It initiates a dialogue which enables both partners in the contract to comment and *reflect*, in a productive and positive way, upon what's *actually* happening in the classroom.

I have tried to put the contract into its place in the organization of learning in Fig. 2, p. 28. The figure helps to remind us that the contract is a reflection (or meeting-ground) of two influences: it's a contract that seeks to include the child as a fellow-negotiator of what happens in the drama; it carries the possibility of translating the view of learning and the view of drama outlined in the Introduction into practice.

Fig. 2 The place of the drama contract in the organization of learning

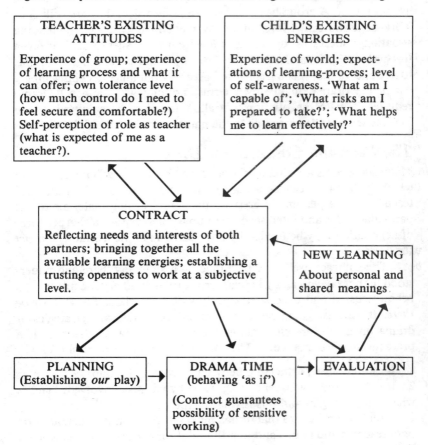

TEACHER'S EXISTING ATTITUDES

Experience of group; experience of learning process and what it can offer; own tolerance level (how much control do I need to feel secure and comfortable?) Self-perception of role as teacher (what is expected of me as a teacher?).

CHILD'S EXISTING ENERGIES

Experience of world; expectations of learning-process; level of self-awareness. 'What am I capable of'; 'What risks am I prepared to take?'; 'What helps me to learn effectively?'

CONTRACT

Reflecting needs and interests of both partners; bringing together all the available learning energies; establishing a trusting openness to work at a subjective level.

NEW LEARNING

About personal and shared meanings

PLANNING
(Establishing *our* play)

DRAMA TIME
(behaving 'as if')

(Contract guarantees possibility of sensitive working)

EVALUATION

The Terms of the Learning Contract

This section outlines graphically (Fig. 3, pp. 29–31) the variety of terms necessary to establish the appropriate learning climate in drama. I have tried to express them in such a way that they honour the learner as much as the teacher and reflect the power-sharing nature of the drama contract. I have also tried to indicate the kind of terms that need to be thought about, and the kind of purpose served by the clusters of terms. There is, of course, considerable overlap between the terms and the list is not intended to be exhaustive – nor is it entirely satisfactory; but it serves as a focus for considering the nature of the learning contract needed for drama. It's not suggested that *all* the terms must be held in the mind simultaneously (the contract will probably evolve organically as and when its terms are needed) or be thrown up in discussion, or emerge in the work. It's important to see the contract as a dynamic process rather than as a passive pact that is laid down and left unchanged. In order to keep the contract as a lively and useful challenge to both partners, the teacher needs to be in a constant state of negotiation, and to know which strategies are needed to put the contract into practice.

Fig. 3   The terms of the learning contract

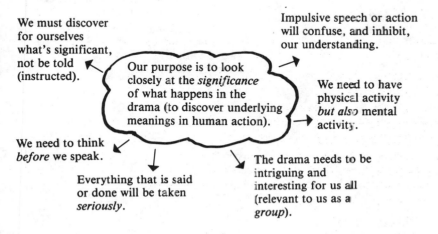

We must discover for ourselves what's significant, not be told (instructed).

Impulsive speech or action will confuse, and inhibit, our understanding.

Our purpose is to look closely at the *significance* of what happens in the drama (to discover underlying meanings in human action).

We need to have physical activity *but also* mental activity.

We need to think *before* we speak.

Everything that is said or done will be taken *seriously*.

The drama needs to be intriguing and interesting for us all (relevant to us as a group).

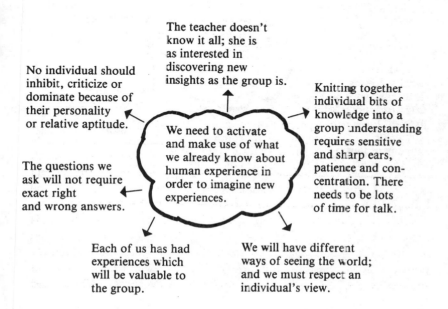

No individual should inhibit, criticize or dominate because of their personality or relative aptitude.

The teacher doesn't know it all; she is as interested in discovering new insights as the group is.

Knitting together individual bits of knowledge into a group understanding requires sensitive and sharp ears, patience and concentration. There needs to be lots of time for talk.

We need to activate and make use of what we already know about human experience in order to imagine new experiences.

The questions we ask will not require exact right and wrong answers.

Each of us has had experiences which will be valuable to the group.

We will have different ways of seeing the world; and we must respect an individual's view.

29

If the teacher is willing to view us as individuals, then the teacher must be respected as an individual (no using drama to mess the teacher up).

We will stop the work from touching 'raw nerves' or getting 'too close to the bone'.

We need to feel safe in what we do.

If the task is too demanding, we will voice our concerns appropriately rather than avoiding the issue through negative or mock-apathetic behaviour.

We need to decide *together* what's possible for us.

Our contributions must be protected against ironic jibes or mickey-taking.

Personal feuds and prejudices must be suspended for the drama. We *must* give people the chance to be somebody else.

We haven't automatically given permission to be stared at by others. (There must be a bond of trust with the audience.)

We need to make the most of our strengths and help each other to overcome weaknesses.

We need to feel confident and respected if we are to progress.

We will describe what successes and failures we have – but we cannot work freely if there is competition, grading or marks for technique.

Our contributions must be valued and acted on by the teacher (implicitly or explicitly).

Questioning needs to be gentle probing, rather than threatening exposure of ignorance.

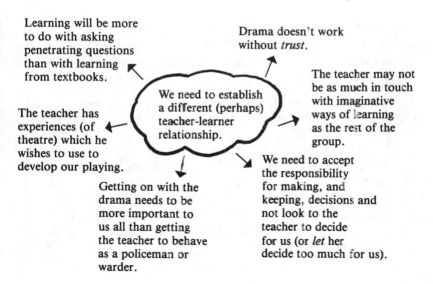

Learning will be more to do with asking penetrating questions than with learning from textbooks.

The teacher has experiences (of theatre) which he wishes to use to develop our playing.

Drama doesn't work without *trust*.

The teacher may not be as much in touch with imaginative ways of learning as the rest of the group.

We need to establish a different (perhaps) teacher-learner relationship.

Getting on with the drama needs to be more important to us all than getting the teacher to behave as a policeman or warder.

We need to accept the responsibility for making, and keeping, decisions and not look to the teacher to decide for us (or *let* her decide too much for us).

Putting the Terms in Order

The priority which a teacher gives to the terms of the contract, and the way in which she negotiates (or signals) the terms to her group, will indicate to them the nature of the learning encounter. Children are generally very sharp when it comes to deciphering what's on offer in a particular teacher's classroom – they have to be, in order to survive. So it makes sense for the teacher to spend time considering the priority she is going to give to certain terms, particularly if she is going to be working over a long period of time with the same group: what should be the initial terms to be put across? how will the priorities reflect a group's (or teacher's) development?

The most important consequence of the way in which the teacher allocates priorities in her contract will be to signal to the children whose agenda will operate during the lesson. By paying attention to the teacher's language, questioning, decision-making, forms of individual and group negotiation, and her expectations of the group, the children will be able to tell whether the agenda is to be decided completely by the teacher, decided in consultation with the group, or left to the group to decide. (Next time you have the chance to observe your own, or somebody else's teaching, listen for the priority signals – it can be a very revealing activity! Being aware of how our priorities are established in the classrooms helps us to check that there is a match between what we *actually* do and say and what we *think* we are doing.)

31

A Note of Caution

Before we go on to deal in more detail with strategies for drama work, here are three cautions to prevent an overzealous persual of the contract approach!

1   The contract is central, it is a prerequisite; *but* drama will be a fairly tedious chore if endless amounts of time are spent discussing the contract terms (i.e. nit-picking!).

2   There are always two sides to a contract and from time to time the teacher may well fail to observe it. It's not there just to remind learners what's needed!

3   The contract must not become a crutch – there is a lot more to drama beyond the contract and, as a result, not all problems will stem from it. If I teach a thoroughly boring lesson, it's no use me accusing a disinterested class of failing to keep the contract!

References

JACKSON, D. (1982) *Continuity in Secondary English* (Methuen)

VYGOTSKY, L. S. (1976) 'Play and its role in the mental development of the child' in Bruner, Jolly and Sylva (eds.) *Play: Its Role in Development and Evolution* (Penguin)

chapter 4

Forms of Negotiation

A Subtle Tongue

The most important tool for a drama teacher is a 'subtle tongue'. I apologize for the vagueness of that term, but in my experience effective teachers are those who have learnt their own meaning of 'subtle tongue'; they are at the opposite end of the spectrum from teachers who habitually employ an ironic tongue, usually with devastating effect!

I will draw out the uses of the subtle tongue in drama work in a moment, but it might be worth turning to the dictionary to help us pin down the subtle–ironic contrast. Under *irony* we find: 'Subtle (*sic*) mockery or humour; sarcasm; way of speaking in which words mean the opposite of their normal or apparent meaning'. (It's worth remembering that not only is irony a potentially cruel device, it is also seldom mastered, or used, by children until they themselves are adult.) Under *subtle* we find: 'Delicate; not obvious; elusive; keenly intelligent or perceptive; ingenious; clever, cunning'. In drama, it is often necessary to develop all those meanings in our teaching, even if some of them appear at first to be inappropriate teaching terms. I hope what follows will help you see them in a teaching context.

'Delicate'

It's probably clear by now that drama depends upon the building of *trust* in classroom relationships, and the degree of that trust will stem, in part, from a growing sense of individual self-esteem. In order to achieve this, a teacher's language needs to be carefully considered and directed towards developing confidence in children. It needs to be a language that encourages and stimulates, rather than inhibits, language use by children.

'Not Obvious'

It's important for children to develop their own opinions and feelings in the drama rather than temporarily 'borrow' the teacher's. In discussion work we are often frustrated by the feeling that children are telling us what they think we want to hear from them, rather than voicing their own opinions. When those same children find themselves sunk into a drama, faced with an actual situation that tests their opinions, they often articulate very different points of view from those heard in the discussion (as long as the teacher has avoided indicating too strongly her own feelings and opinions).

As an example, let us take a class who were working on the theme of 'outsiders'. They had discussed immigrants, gypsies, ex-convicts etc. and dutifully agreed that we should be understanding, kind and tolerant towards outsiders. A week later, however, they took on the roles of villagers in a cosy, trusting village where it was safe to leave doors unlocked. At a meeting they heard of plans to turn an empty building into a 'halfway home' for prisoners who had served their time (i.e. already been punished). The ensuing outrage was most illuminating for the teacher, particularly when it was suggested that the ex-prisoners should be permanently tattooed! As a result, the teacher found a way, through drama, of helping children to discover the implications of that attitude from *within the context of a situation* rather than by instructing them as to what the appropriate attitude (in her view) *should* be.

'*Elusive*'

The teacher's purpose in drama is to make the children do all the work! If children ask us questions, it's much less tiring for us to give an answer than to help children discover the answer for themselves. It takes energy to help children 'learn how to learn', but it's energy well spent! In order to demonstrate that there are resources of knowledge other than the teacher, it may sometimes be necessary to adopt an elusive attitude.

'*Keenly Intelligent or Perceptive*'

It is important to register not just what is being said by children, but also what lies *behind* what is being said; and also to be aware of what is not being said but might be with some subtle coaxing on the teacher's part! One of the aims in drama is to change the level of a group's thinking – to move beyond the surface of actions. In order to do this, a teacher has to discover a mode of language that will be accessible to children and yet which will also challenge them to search for meanings that may be deeply embedded in the drama.

The following dialogue occurred during a lesson on Red Indians with a group of nine-year-olds. Earlier in the drama, they had considered a real peace-pipe and made suggestions as to what it meant to the tribe it belonged to.

T Teacher; B Boy; G Girl; C Chorus.

T I asked you to come and sit over here as if you were Indians. Why did you come and sit in a circle-shape?

B That's how Indians sit.

B They always sit in circles.

T So when you think of Indians, you think of them sitting here like this in a circle?

G Yes.

T Do you think the circle is important to the Indians?

G Yes . . . I think so.

T I wonder why that is? Who knows a reason?

B Because of the fire.

T Yes.

B The fire's in the middle so everyone keeps warm, no one is left out.

T Is the circle to do with the importance of sharing then?

C Yes.

B It's easier to pass round the peace-pipe when you're in a circle, you just pass it to who's sitting next to you.

T Yes. Any other reasons we can think of?

G You can see whoever is talking when you're in a circle.

T Yes, like now you can see whoever talks now.

G Nobody is different.

T That's interesting. Do you want to explain that a bit further?

G Well, we're all the same, nobody is higher or lower or anything like that.

T What about the Chief?

B Yes, but he sits in the circle with us.

T So, might that mean that everyone from the highest to the lowest has a valuable place in our tribe, and will be heard?

(*Nods*)

T What else might this circle mean to our tribe? Is there anything special about the circle-shape; just the shape of it?

(*Confused looks!*)

T Well, how is it different to a straight line or a square, for instance?

B It hasn't got corners.

G Or edges.

G It doesn't . . .

T Yes?

G It doesn't finish or end.

B It doesn't begin either.

T It has no beginning or ending, is that right?

(*Nods*)

T   Might that be important to us?
C   Yes.
T   Why?
G   It might mean that our tribe has no beginning or ending, it lasts
    forever.

'Cunning'

New learning is often created by a disturbance, and in drama a teacher
sometimes plays devil's advocate or takes a provocative stance in order
to challenge or draw out a response. A teacher deliberately throwing a
spanner in the works often stimulates a group into mental, linguistic and
physical action! If everybody agrees the motorway should be built, then
the teacher goes against it; the teacher adopts a cunning strategy in order
to introduce some tension into the action. Cunning is also required
sometimes in order to work around a problem, or to bring a group into a
new relationship with a problem. If a group feels too inhibited to enter a
drama directly, the teacher may need her subtle-cunning to find ways of
introducing them indirectly: 'Well, if *you* were in that situation what
would *you* say to us?' (i.e. how would *you* deal with it as *yourself*, not in
role? Let's find a more comfortable way of edging in).

Questions

Skilful questioning is likely to be one of the drama teacher's most useful tools.
At the beginning of a lesson, questions can be used to establish the context of
the drama; during the lesson to involve the participants and to deepen and
focus their thinking; and after the lesson, to reflect upon and evaluate the
experience.... Most teachers' questions are a way of gaining information, of
checking facts... too often the 'correct' answer already exists in the teachers'
minds... Questioning in drama will have a very different purpose from
this.... In drama, there is no right answer. The teacher is not asking questions
to which there is a single appropriate response. (O'Neill and Lambert)

Questions are both the material and the negotiating medium of
drama. Drama is an investigative form; it is concerned with probing
questions raised (by the content) about some aspect of human
experience: what would happen if? what would it be like if? what would
we do if? what does it mean to be in this situation? In order to focus on
these broad questions, the teacher leads the group's enquiry through
more manageable and structured questions designed to focus and clarify
their thinking.

It's my feeling that drama's appeal as a learning medium to both
learners and teachers is partly to do with its interactive and concrete
nature and partly also to do with the form of its questions which are seen
as being open-ended, consequential, originating from a shared curiosity

about our immediate environment and other environments which are beyond our actual experience. Children enjoy finding out *if* they sense the possibility of *discovering* what's possible for themselves, rather than feeling that 'what's possible' has already been decided, prescribed and defined by the teacher acting as instructor or high-priest of knowledge. The possibility of enjoyment in learning is there in drama because the questions it addresses itself to cannot be known in a passive received way. Drama as a way into history often stumbles in this respect. Recently I worked with a class who were looking at the question of succession in 1066. My open-ended enquiry was to do with the shifting attitudes and self-interest amongst the Witan (the bishops and earls who decided on Harold). It was a non-starter for the group because the story was *known-fact* – there was no possibility of arriving at our own alternative account; *the facts of history were immutable.* What I should have done was to work through an analogous situation where there was a possibility of the group working towards a number of alternative conclusions, i.e. in the same situation of flux that the Witan were actually in (which is the experience the children wanted).

Kinds of Questions

Most accounts of drama deal in detail with the varieties of question-approaches a teacher uses both in setting up the drama and also during the drama itself (in role). Below I have used these accounts to develop a grid of kinds of questions and examples of questions.

MODE OF QUESTION	EXAMPLES	PURPOSE
Seeking information	What shall we do a play about? What sort of a place is this? How many of us should go? Where will we go for help? Does this happen at night or in the day? What would we look like? etc.	This is our play
Containing information	Are you sure we have everything we need? How long will it take us, on horses? What else will we carry, apart from our weapons?	I want to *suggest* what's needed, not tell.

MODE OF QUESTION	EXAMPLES	PURPOSE
Provoking research	What did ships look like in those days? How does a nuclear reactor work? Do we know enough about the Victorians to start? How did the Vikings manage to make boots without using nails? What would happen if we mixed these chemicals together?	We need to know more about this before we go on.
Controlling	Do you want to continue with this play or not? Are we prepared to listen to each other? Is this the way Indians would behave? How can the king hear us if we all talk at once? What's the best way of organizing ourselves?	It's important that we realize that drama is a controlled demanding activity – not playing around.
Branching	Shall we be in the past, present or future? Are we all men, or mixed? Do you want to work as individuals, or in families? Are we rich or poor? Do you want to be frightened by this stranger, or do we trust her? Are we going to camp here or go a bit further?	We need to decide between alternative courses of action.
Seeking opinions	What did you feel about the teacher-role? What might happen next? What other ways might there be of looking at that situation? Do you feel	I want to know about how it is for you, individually.

MODE OF QUESTION	EXAMPLES	PURPOSE
	comfortable with this way of working? What do *you* think of when you think of Indians? How much choice do you want in what we do?	
Encouraging reflection	I wonder what makes a person want to go to space? I wonder what sort of leader we will need? How would you act under this pressure? What do you find you must have, you cannot live without? Can you find the words to express what you feel at this moment? As we stand here, I wonder what each of us might be thinking?	It's important for us to think about what this means to us.

The Language of Questions

If a question is to be a genuinely 'freeing' question rather than a closed one, careful attention needs to be paid to the language in which the question is framed. 'Freeing' questions don't begin:

Don't you agree that ...?
Don't you think that ...?
Wouldn't you rather ...?
Wouldn't you like to ...?
It seems to me that we should ... don't you agree?

The most effective 'freeing' questions are often framed as pondering, musing, supposing questions that invite assistance from the group:

Can anyone see how we're going to get out of this?
I can't make any sense of this, can you?
I just can't imagine ...
I've often wondered ...
Well I'm stuck, has anybody else got any thoughts?
Supposing ... what might happen then?

The most important distinction between these types of questions is that the second group try to avoid indicating that the teacher is looking for a particular answer or that a value will be placed on certain answers from the range offered by the children.

Coping with Answers

The problem is that if you learn the knack of effective questioning, then you will find yourself being offered a rich variety of answers! Those answers may be divergent, idiosyncratic, seemingly disconnected, indicative of a range of levels of thinking – or just plain difficult to accommodate. The contract states clearly that you will value every well-intentioned contribution that is made; so just how will you manage not to offend, or put down, a contributor by undervaluing (not acting-on) her answer?

The strategies that I will suggest here may be contentious and so I will need to place them first within the context of the form of bargaining that is appropriate to drama.

Drama is a *collective* activity; it involves people working together with a more-or-less single purpose. Whereas in children's other art-work such as drawing, writing stories, reading stories and poetry we consciously encourage and prize *individual* ideas and expression, in drama we encourage a collective view, a conspectus, a commonality of expression. This is not to say we are content with achieving a consensus (which usually means agreeing to evade differences or divisions of opinion in order to find the 'safe' middle ground). Conspectus is a more accurate term in that it conveys the sense of a synopsis of opinions, in other words there may be a wide range of opinions (and differences) reflected in the drama – and certainly the drama will seek to encompass each individual's view. In drama, then, we are saying to children that although we are working together as a group, individual reactions and opinions are still important; what we need to do is to see whether our individual ideas can be meshed, or patterned, into an experience that we can share together. The teacher's role then is to look for possibilities of grouping answers, to look for patterns that establish a conspectus whilst not ignoring or leaving out 'rogue' answers that don't seem to fit at first. The following strategies might help:

1 *Teacher writing answers down* The contributor feels her answer is important enough to be recorded; it creates a space between answers (it takes time to write them down!); as a group we can consider the collected answers and look for patterns; we can come back to the answers later on and reconsider them.

2 *Small-group talk prior to offering answers to the whole group* We

can test out our answers on our friends first; everybody gets a chance to talk; we can redefine our answer in the light of conversations with others; I may not speak in front of everybody but I feel safe with my friend; I'm confident that there are others who share my opinion.

3 *Withholding the teacher response* This involves simply collecting answers from the group *without* commenting on each one *until* all the available answers have been voiced; each answer is accepted without an implicit or explicit value being placed on it; the teacher is seen as recorder rather than arbitrator of opinions; the teacher can sense the variety and differences in *all* the answers before deciding how to proceed; the children are not inhibited by fear of what the teacher might say, i.e. are more likely to give public voice to their ideas.

4 *Gentle encouragement to the shy!* I know you've got your hand up, but you've done a lot of the work so far. I'm worried that we haven't yet heard from some of the others. I'm wondering what you might be thinking over there – is there anybody who *hasn't* spoken yet, who would like to answer now?; also selecting from a forest of hands someone who rarely contributes.

5 *Looking for common themes; recurring answers* We are being asked to consider whether our viewpoint has anything in common with other viewpoints expressed; are we giving the same kind of answers? can we see any general feelings emerging? are we prepared to accept a group decision? how important is it for me to go against the others?

Voting

Voting is the way democracies decide, and on the surface it may seem a fair way of deciding in drama. *But*, again, voting shouldn't be a way of avoiding basic differences amongst the group. If 20 are for it, and five are against that is one thing, but if 13 are for it and 12 against, the teacher will need to work out a form of proportional representation in order to be fair to both interests.

Although these crucially important forms of negotiation will be constantly at work throughout the lesson the forms will manifest in different ways according to the different activity the group are engaged in. Some of the negotiating will be about our actual situation as teachers and learners in this classroom, at this time – the *actual phase* if you like. (I use 'phase' here in the sense as defined in the dictionary of 'stage or form in a *cycle* of growth or change'.) Some of the negotiating will occur when we are behaving (pretending) 'as if' we were other people, in another place at another time – the *'as if' phase*. Some of the negotiation will occur as we look back and evaluate our experiences in both the actual and the 'as if' phases – the *reflective phase*. The next chapter

41

looks closely at these different phases and the ways in which the forms of negotiation discussed here manifest themselves in each phase.

Reference

O'NEILL, C. and LAMBERT, A. (1982) *Drama Structures* (Hutchinson)

chapter 5
Phases of Negotiation

So that we can look more closely at the way the possibilities for learning develop as the drama session moves along, I am going to divide drama artificially into three distinct phases: planning, drama-time and evaluation. I am not suggesting, however, that it is always possible to divide up what goes on in a drama session in such a neat way; nor am I suggesting that equal weight in terms of time and value should be given to the three categories. Some sessions may seem like planning with brief periods of drama-time, and some may seem like all drama-time with very little planning – it's not what you do, it's the way that you do it! I will look closest at *drama-time* because planning and evaluation have both been mentioned, and will be mentioned again later.

Planning – What Might Happen
The purpose of the negotiation in the planning phase is to establish the *nature* of the three-way relationship represented below:

LEARNING MATERIALS

In the traditional transmission model of teaching the relationship often appears like this:

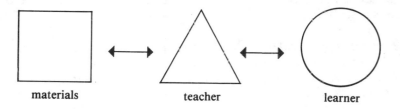

materials   teacher   learner

In other words the teacher stands between the learning material and the learner and transmits (and decides) what is to be learnt. The awful tragedy of this model is that the learner is never allowed to get to grips with the material itself. The teacher's view is that her children don't know enough to be able to deal with the material *directly*.

In drama (and other areas of the curriculum too) we do *not* share this view. We are planning to find ways of activating what children *do* know so as to place them in a more direct relationship with the learning material. This does not always mean simply standing out of the way and letting children get on with it. It usually means providing a form which will act as a *focussing lens* for the children to look through to the material beyond. In drama these lenses (there are as many as our imaginations can conceive) are usually some form of dramatic action. In other classrooms they may be a story, a poem, a piece of music, a drawing. Whatever is chosen it must be a strong enough structure to hold the children's interest; and they must be able to see a clear *intention* and *purpose* in it. It's no good providing lenses that don't help us to see for ourselves!

In the planning phase, then, we are establishing this kind of relationship:

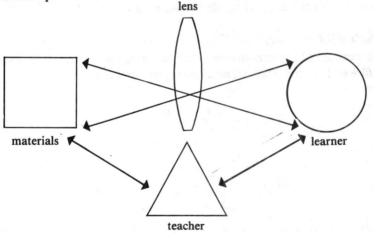

and also trying to achieve a necessary balance between various states or roles described below.

Teacher ←→ Learner (The contract)

Is this material something we can *all* be interested in?

In what sort of ways (lenses) would it be useful for us to look at this material?

What are we interested in finding out from this material?
What do we expect from each other during this lesson?

Familiar ←→ *Unfamiliar (Preparing the middle ground)*

What do we already know about this material?
Are there any actual experiences we have had that might help us into this new territory?
What resources (cultural or classroom) do we have (or will we need) at our disposal?
What sort of imagined experience will we feel safe and confident about working in?
Will we need to practise anything before we start?
How can we establish our belief in what we're doing?

Teacher-Focus ←→ *Children's Focus (Foreground)*

What 'bits' of the material (experience) are we interested in bracketing-off to look at closely?
What are we going to pay closest attention to?
What aspect of this experience interests us most/will be most profitable for us to explore?
Out of all this material what will we place in the *foreground*?

Action ←→ *Reflection (Locking-in to the theme)*

At what level of seriousness are we going to work?
How might the action we're planning reveal the theme?
What balance between doing and thinking will best suit us, and our purpose?
What might prevent us from becoming involved with this theme?
How can we best structure the action so that the thinking becomes part of the doing?
We need to be clear about what we are looking at and not stray away from it in our planning.

Game ←→ *Theatre (Finding-form)*

What will the rules (conventions) of the game (play) be?
What ways of working will we be using?
How will the various roles identified function together as a team (ensemble)?
What is the nature (tension) of this particular game (play) – is it: a puzzle? hide and seek? winning/competing? being trapped/losing? choosing/risking? blocking/deceiving? rewarding/punishing?
In what ways can theatre-form help to deepen (make significant) the level of our playing?

The planning stage of the drama lesson will resemble conventional classroom activity – the space will be arranged, the teacher may use the blackboard, the children will refer to teacher as 'Miss' or 'Sir', instructions may be given, discussion will be going on. It's a period of preparation. There will be a sense of something different about to happen. The class is getting ready to go into drama-time.

Drama-Time – What Is Happening

Some forms of drama-time may appear to be much the same as what 'normally' goes on in the classroom. In other words, it may be that the teacher has told the group what to do and they go and do it; or that the teacher is controlling what's going on from the front – she's 'telling' the class what to do. But the learning contract promises something different – a change in the normal dynamics of the classroom. It also creates the conditions for the class to move beyond the actual resources present in a classroom. The opportunity is there for the class and teacher to step into imagined contexts 'as if' they were actually (authentically) happening to them, i.e. to suspend the reality of the classroom context in order to pretend, as a group, that they are *other* people, in *another* place, in *another* time. (Of course working inside an imagined context is not the only activity we will find in drama-time. Many other activities might go on which help a group to prepare, or deepen, their response to the imagined context, activities which will help a group 'edge-in' to the dramatic context so that they have enough emotional material and sense of purpose to get the most from their role-play within the imagined context.) The focus here is on looking at the extra forms of negotiation made available to a teacher and group once they move from the actual dimensions of the classroom into the imagined dimensions of a dramatic context (a play).

Working in Role

It's important to remember that the experience of drama-time will be *fundamentally* different for learners as compared to the teacher. Whereas the learners' conventional role will be substantially changed by the dramatic context, i.e. they will be negotiating 'as if' they were a mayor, a villager, a warrior rather than negotiating as 'children-at-school', the teacher's role does not change: she will be negotiating as *teacher* (with a learning purpose in mind) even though she may appear to the group to be negotiating as mayor, villager, or warrior. This device of appearing to be involved in the dramatic context in the same way as the children, whilst actually being involved as teacher, is a particularly effective one for allowing the teacher to stand out of the children's way in order to give them a more direct view of the learning material through the lens of the dramatic context they are all involved in (see Fig. 4, below). (The purpose of this device is also of course to alter the normative power relationship in learning. The teacher's purpose is to place the group in an active relationship with the learning material so that she may help them to make sense for themselves rather than remain in a position where she will be expected by convention to 'give sense' to her group.)

Fig. 4 The teacher's position and purpose in drama-time

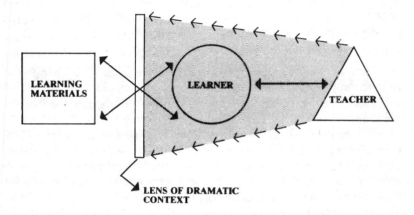

LEARNING MATERIALS

LEARNER

TEACHER

LENS OF DRAMATIC CONTEXT

In order to look closely at how 'teacher-in-role' works as a form of negotiation, and in particular how it can be used to initiate a drama, it will be necessary to deal with other aspects of the device as well.

Using Role to Start the Drama

I am constantly amazed by the miracle of how thinking (planning) about a dramatic idea can in an instant become that of carrying it into action. There is a world of difference between someone in a class saying, 'Well, they should take all their belongings with them' and saying, 'Let's pack up and leave'. That is the *switch* I work for, to enable a dramatic expression of ideas to take place. (Heathcote)

This switch isn't an easy 'on/off' affair! The change of tense from 'would' to 'is' is an immediate indication that the group has moved into drama-time: but it may take longer for everybody to believe in the pretence; see its possibilities; adjust to new roles; feel enough commitment to contribute; recognize the language and behaviour that will be appropriate to the pretence (i.e. will give it credibility). It's like opening a book and reading a story. It takes a while for a reader to lose her consciousness of the actual surroundings she is reading in, get over the mechanics of manipulating the pages and the print and begin to be drawn into the story, until eventually she is lost in it, in a different state.

The same is true of starting a drama – the group often need to be 'led' into the action *by* the teacher. It's easier for the group (and less personally demanding and threatening) if the teacher herself indicates that the group is moving into drama-time by taking a role in the drama, and if, also *she uses that role as a way of inviting and helping the group to assume, or recognize, their imagined roles*. The teacher suddenly talking and behaving 'as-if' she was someone else isn't going to work as an immediate switch for the group either – there's more to it than that – but teacher-in-role is a very efficient way of starting the drama.

By introducing the drama in role, the teacher is:

1   offering the class a model of role-play, in particular she is giving signs as to the appropriate language and level of seriousness.

2   demonstrating the 'naturalness' of being in role (giving confidence to the group).

3   offering the group an invitation to join her in the drama if they want.

4   indicating, by addressing the group 'as-if' they were other than themselves and she were 'other' than teacher, that the normal dynamics and relationships of the classroom have been suspended (i.e. it's not teacher that the children will be dealing with).

5   creating the chance of informing the group through a wider system of signing than would be possible just as teacher. She can communicate meanings to the group through posture, register, tone, silences, a symbolic use of space and objects. She isn't restricted to direct telling as is often the case in actual teaching.

Drama Isn't Actual – It's Fictional

There must be no confusion in the drama between what is actual and what is fictional. The teacher must make it perfectly clear to all that she is starting a *fiction*, a make-believe – it is not real. She must also make it clear that she is adopting a fictional role – she is being 'other' than her real self.

Because drama feels so concrete and practical, teachers are sometimes tempted to introduce situations and roles as if they were *really* happening to the children: 'We've just had a phone call from the police saying there's a bomb in the school – don't panic'; 'I've just broken my arm in the playground, can anyone help me?' Sensitive drama work depends on trust – it's important for the children to feel secure that the teacher isn't going to play this kind of con trick with them. It makes life very confusing if you are unsure of what is real and what is not; the teacher's purpose is not to confuse but to make clear. Apart from being potentially dangerous, a 'this-is-for-real' approach results in the children devoting large amounts of their thinking energy to trying to sort out the actual from the fictional. There are more productive uses in drama for that energy; it's needed for penetrating the meanings offered in the *fiction* of the drama. Making it clear to the children when they are in drama-time and when they are not, when the teacher is in role and when she is not, doesn't in any way weaken the participants' response to the drama. We can be completely involved as we read a book and learn from our involvement with it; it is just as possible to become involved at a deep level with a fiction offered by drama, and to learn from our involvement with that.

Co-authorship in the Drama

Although drama is not story, there are interesting comparisons between the way 'meanings' are constructed in both story and drama. In a sense, the teacher is using role to start 'writing' the drama. She is consciously selecting phrases and actions for the children to 'read', and then offering them the chance to use role in order to 'write' themselves into the action. Because the teacher is trying to work *indirectly* (i.e. at an affective rather than just at an intellectual level), the 'writing' is suggestive and resonant, offering a number of open-ended possibilities to which the group can respond. For the child, it's like registering the clues offered in a good story when expectations are aroused by familiar signs. Compare the way Philippa Pearce uses sign to indirectly suggest possibilities in her opening to *The Battle of Bubble and Squeak* with an equally indirect opening to a drama.

1   The middle of the night, and everyone in the house asleep. Everyone? Then what was that noise? CREAK! and then, after a pause, CREAK! And then CREAK! As regular as clockwork – but was this just clockwork? Behind the creaking, the lesser sound of some delicate tool working on metal.

2   (The children are standing in two lines facing each other, with a space between them. At the head of the lines, the teacher has placed two chairs, one slightly higher than the other; on the lower chair is a 'crown'. The teacher enters through the lines and stands in front of the higher chair. After a pause he says:) 'Great scribes and priests, it is with much displeasure that we learn that you have refused to obey the instructions of our new wife, your queen, to remove the idols which she finds so heathen to her faith, from your temples. What have you to say for yourselves? We are here to listen to your excuses.'

The difference of course is that the drama example offers the 'readers' the chance to become involved in the *action* and to share in the 'writing' of the drama with the teacher. This is the unique opportunity of drama; that children can be involved in it, with others, reading and writing as they go along. They are in effect acting as co-authors under the teacher's editorial guidance.

Controlling the Teacher Role

The teacher's handling of role will be crucial in ensuring that the group don't just follow teacher, but genuinely share in the writing. If the drama becomes an ego-trip for 'Miss', then the children won't feel able to get in on the action for themselves. The role needs to be enough to get things started and to act as a strong focus for the class's interest, but it needs to be subtle enough to place the group in a position where they will have to make the next move. In the 'Beowulf' session, for instance, the teacher immediately invites the group to relate anecdotes in context. The children may not, of course, automatically grasp the opportunity to respond! The teacher may have to stop almost immediately if nothing is forthcoming, and discuss with the group what sort of responses and alternative courses of action there are. They may, through inhibition, collapse into giggles, thus making it necessary to stop and try again.

But it's also important to remember that the purpose of using teacher-role is to put the *children* into an immediate situation where they have to do the thinking, the talking, the responding, the decision-taking, the problem-solving. It's often hard for us as teachers to step back from our class when they are dealing with a problem; we want to wade in, help them sort it out, show them the right approach. In drama it's essential, whenever possible, to step back and push the group into using their own combined resources as a way of dealing with whatever arises. The teacher should deliberately withhold her expertise and knowledge even if that means long embarrassing pauses while the group figure out what to say or do for themselves; it must be the children's work.

In order for this to happen, the teacher-role should never be over-powering and obviously manipulative, *it should try not to talk too much*, and its contribution should be cut back to a few, well-considered, highly selective phrases or actions each designed to activate responses *from* the children.

When the teacher-in-role is responding to questions asked by the group, she should try to avoid just giving straight information – the teacher's response needs to be framed in such a way that it will provoke further responses from the children. It's the important difference between answering the question, 'Is your house haunted?' with 'Yes, it is, the ghost of my grandfather walks here, he was murdered by . . .' and

'It's had a troubled history, this house, there is some talk about it in the village, rumours and gossip'.

The teacher-in-role not only has the responsibility of bringing the whole group into the drama, but also the further responsibility of working individuals into the drama. This means looking out for individuals who are having difficulty believing in it; keeping a balance between the genders, so neither is overpowered by the other; encouraging (without forcing) the quiet and shy to contribute – 'You men over there are very quiet, I wonder what you're thinking?'; assigning roles that will be suitable (and useful) to individuals – 'Who will be my first mate?'

Choosing a Role

The role that the teacher chooses for herself will define the kind of responses the children, in other roles, will make. It will also define their opportunities for making responses and determine a relationship with the group. It helps, when choosing, to have a mental checklist of types of roles and their usefulness. Geoff Gillham has offered the following basic types of role as a guide:

1 **leader – authority role**
2 **opposer – authority role**
3 **the intermediate role**
4 **needing help/victim role**
5 **the lowest status role.**

Let us look at *some* of the possibilities, and limits, of each type.

1 *Leader – authority role* e.g. king, gang-boss, captain, chairperson, mayor etc. A useful type of role for the inexperienced. Allows the teacher to remain firmly in charge of the direction of the drama and the decision-taking, *but* limits opportunity to shed responsibility onto others in the group.

2 *Opposer – authority role* e.g. unjust king, cruel factory-owner, property developer in a beautiful village, dishonest politician, monster, giant. The teacher retains authority but the group is 'gelled' together in opposition to the role, opposition being a motivation for them to respond: 'My company is going to build an industrial complex here in Abbotsford Village'. *But* it's difficult to move the drama in any other direction once a relationship based on opposition has been established.

3 *The intermediate role* e.g. messenger, emissary, 'on-duty-at-the-time' policeman, foreman, doctor's assistant, first officer following orders. This is the most versatile and useful type of role. The teacher is not in direct authority, but acts as a link between others of higher and lower status; she can pass on information and give children in the group

the responsibility for dealing with that information and framing a response to it: 'The captain says we're to keep going – rations are to be cut to make our food last'; 'The king says the taxes must go up to pay for his new castle'; 'I have been sent to ask whether you will sign the treaty'. *But* the teacher is taking more risks than with the authority roles, and the group need to be able to handle the responsibility offered by this type of role; it is less easy to prevent the children forming splinter-groups.

4 *Needing help/victim role* e.g. unfunny clown, slave, gypsy, persecuted villager, scapegoat, illiterate immigrant. The teacher is asking for help from the group; this places them in a position of responsibility and power in relation to the teacher as their status is raised above their actual status as pupils. This is particularly useful for low-ability groups and offers them a sense of achievement if they can help the role. *But* it requires considerable skill on the teacher's part – she has no direct control over the group and they may have difficulty organizing themselves effectively.

5 *The lowest status role* e.g. slave, villager, member of the crew, workers, servant, young person. The teacher is working from the bottom of the pile; she may be negotiating with children in authority or high-status roles thus offering them a significantly different order of experience from their conventional classroom experience. Children are often very drawn to this type of role which is useful for working *inside* the group, as one of the crowd, rather than at a distance as someone special (authority role). Responsibility is shared amongst the group. *But* there is the same problem of control as with the victim role, i.e. a danger of over-influencing the attitude of the group the role is a part of.

Evaluation – What Has Happened

The problem with separating planning, drama-time, evaluation from each other is that it suggests a sequence – a smooth moving through from one stage to another. This is not what happens in practice where there is more likely to be a shifting to and fro between different forms of activity. It's likely that the opening of a lesson will be concerned with planning; that some drama-time will probably follow; and that there will be some evaluative talk towards the end of the lesson. But it's also possible that the teacher might offer a few brief explanatory words, go straight into drama-time, stop quickly, ask for an evaluation of what's happening, plan with the group the next development, go back into drama-time etc. Sometimes it's necessary to drop in and out of each kind of activity several times over in order to make the most of a particularly complex situation. So we should expect to see evaluation as an ongoing activity that is returned to throughout the lesson.

Evaluation may take different forms according to its purpose. It may be built into drama-time, i.e. letters home, working as reporters, archivists, historians, tableaux etc.; it may be a conscious standing back from the drama in order to discuss what's happening as ourselves.

Evaluation-in-role keeps the drama going and allows the children to evaluate from within. Evaluation as 'ourselves' allows the children to address themselves to a wider context than just the context of the drama – they are able to discuss other aspects of what's happening in relation to the drama, and also it allows evaluation of the way the drama is developing. In particular there can be open discussion about the nature of the teacher-in-role and the fiction that she is offering: Is it fair? Do you feel you're being pushed in a particular direction? Is it relevant to you? How does it compare with your expectations?

Some Reasons for Evaluation

The decision to move the group into some form of evaluative activity may be inspired by some of the following reasons. Each one might make the teacher think, 'We ought to stop and think and/or talk about this'.

Which direction should we take?

If you're stuck in the drama, or there are a number of possibilities emerging, it makes sense to stop and ask the group what to do. After all, it's their play as well!

Are we missing the significance of what's happening?

You will be trying to draw out the significance from within the drama; but if it's important for the group to register in detail what's happening so that they can respond appropriately, it may be useful to stop and discuss the situation slowly with them.

Are some people lost/confused?

You may find yourself in a situation that is too vague and undefined for the group to be able to work with it; or there may be some frustration because some of the group cannot manage whilst others can.

What other ways are there of looking at this situation?

It may be that a particular approach is obviously failing to release the potential meanings in a situation. Rather than telling the group what these meanings should be, it's better to talk over alternative ways of coming at the situation.

Is this a good place to leave off until next time?

Knowing how to deal with the artificial constraints of school time is a perennial problem for teachers. It's unlikely that the appropriate moment is going to coincide with the bell. A further problem is caused by the need to balance bringing the group out of the 'heat' of the drama, whilst leaving them with enough charged suspense to want to carry on next week. It is best to stop early and evaluate what has happened and where the drama might go next time.

Have we got enough belief/seriousness to work at this?

If you get into the habit of allowing frivolous responses, jokiness, playing about, thoughtless action, self-indulgent behaviour to pass unchecked,you will find yourself with a real problem. There must be an iron discipline to drama work that doesn't *ever* allow that kind of behaviour. At the very first sign you *must* stop the drama and deal with it, though not necessarily in a harsh way – behaviour of this kind may have a range of motives behind it other than 'naughtiness'. *But* the group needs to consider the *necessity* of the terms of the contract before going on.

Is the fiction being too strongly manipulated by teacher?

The teacher will obviously have a strong interest in where the drama goes. She will also have a greater mastery of language and the confidence to be forceful. It is important to check that the group isn't being over-whelmed by the teacher, either being pushed in a direction they might not otherwise take, or developing an attitude based on the teacher's partisan view of an experience. You may also feel that although you have dropped your teacher-tag, the group is still following you – you may need to stop and remind them that they have the chance to challenge and go against the teacher-role in the drama if they wish to.

Is this situation getting too uncomfortable?

The drama may take an unexpected turn and move towards something that you feel is too close for comfort either for you or the group, or particular individuals. In the terms of the contract, there is a guaranteed protection against discomfort. Rather than risking hurt or worry (about our *actual* selves), it's best to stop and make sure everyone's happy to go on, or else how to resume at a distance from the problem area.

Do we want this new idea A has introduced?

It sometimes happens, particularly in the freeflow of a whole-group improvisation, that an individual will want to introduce an idea that will radically alter the direction. The idea might be a very good one that feels right (the king may be offered a poison-cup; a messenger may return with news that the entire 7th Cavalary is about to attack!) but it may be important to stop and discuss the implications of the idea before accepting it.

Is drama-time the most effective way of working?

Drama will not suit every occasion, purpose and problem. You may feel the need to draw, make, read, or write in order to help the group make the most sense out of the learning material they are grappling with. Children have a richer sense than us of the appropriateness of different art-forms; they have little difficulty in switching from one medium to another when it suits their own purpose. We may need reminding by them that we are teachers who use drama, not drama teachers!

Evaluation Out of Drama-time

With older children, it often works better to bring them *out* of drama-time to evaluate in order to deal *directly* with the questions summarized above. Older children tend to be more self-conscious about role-play with the result that they are seldom 'lost' in the drama to the same extent that younger children are. Older children take more of their actual selves into the imagined situation, and so the switch from actual to fictional is not as dramatic (*sic*) for them (they are unlikely to 'role' for long periods for instance). The advantages of actual discussion about the fiction with older children are:

1 You can talk about the dramatic form which holds the situation: 'How did working in mime change the meanings in that situation?'

2 You can establish personal connections with the work: 'John, how was that for you – did you expect that to happen or did it surprise you?'

3 You can signal, explicitly, the kind of teacher/learner relationship available: 'This is an interesting moment, how would you like to see things developing from this point?'

4 You can develop points of view: 'Were the attitudes of the role her attitudes or your own?'

5 You can develop objectification of the subjective experience: 'How would you sum up what's happening in this situation so that it would hold true for someone who's not been here?'

The generalization or assumption contained in this view is that as children enter their mid-teens, they become more interested in their own *personal* meanings – their investment becomes more self-centred. Also, they are now able to control form for *themselves* – they understand how art works. They are becoming more interested in penetrating the construction of drama rather than in being involved in a wholly subjective experience. It's a questionable assumption of course!

In terms of ways of working, it's often more effective to work older children in smaller groups with more choice about what is expressed and how it is expressed. There may be more performance which will create natural breaks for evaluation.

Evaluation in Drama-time

Learning for younger children is more sensual – they learn from 'living' in drama-time. Their understanding of meanings is more likely to be embedded in the imagined experiences of drama-time. They are most effective when they are articulating their understanding from *within* the situation.

So with younger children, evaluation works best when the teacher is able to build it into the drama-time by creating opportunities for the group to stand back from the action and consider it at a deeper and slower level whilst remaining in role. It's the difference between asking the older child, 'What would signing the treaty mean to a tribe of Indians like the Sioux?' and asking the younger child, 'What will signing this treaty mean to our tribe? Let each brave consider how his future will change'.

Many of the suggestions that follow and are developed are to do with shaping drama so that children are placed not just *in* an imagined situation but also *in relation to it*, i.e. in a position where evaluative thought is likely to be generated from *within* the drama. I am not suggesting, however, that evaluation from within the drama is not just as effective for older children, or that evaluation from without is not possible with younger children. There needs to be a balance, but it's a balance that may need to alter as the child develops.

The Place of Evaluation

Drama is metaphor.* Its meaning lies not in the actual amount context nor in the fictitious one, but in the *dialectic* set-up between the two. (Bolton)

Drama is a dialectical, rather than didactic, form of learning. It is to do with drawing out, through open-ended questioning and talk, the consequences for us in our actual lives that have emerged in the imagined world of the fiction: 'What does this play mean for us? What are we to take from it?'

It's not enough to have the experience of drama-time without also having some evaluation centring on the actual-fictional dialectic. By comparing and contrasting the seemingly opposite states of actual-fictional it's possible that we may clarify/modify our understanding of the learning material under scrutiny. In this sense evaluation (in some form) is as essential to learning through drama as drama-time is.

*See Chapter 7, p. 66.

Gavin Bolton identifies the kinds of understanding that may emerge from dialectical evaluation:

1 *Personal* To do with self-understanding and giving new insights into the immediate social environments.

2 *Universal* Using the particular circumstances of the drama to develop a generalization or abstraction. i.e. a play about the Magna Carta may help a group to develop an understanding of abstract notions like freedom, authority, rights.

3 *Analogous* Seeing the connections between the situation in the drama and other situations which seem to be similar, e.g. a space explorer as being in the same situation as Columbus, Shackleton, Scott.

Fig. 5 Drama practice – a review

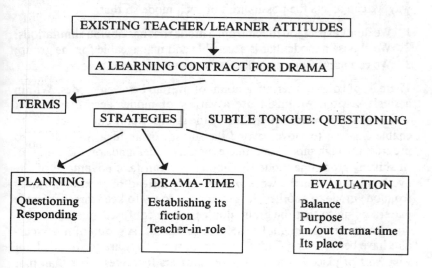

References

BOLTON, G. (1979) *Towards a Theory of Drama in Education* (Longman)

HEATHCOTE, D. (1982) Signs and portents *SCYPT Journal 9*

PEARCE, P. (1981) *The Battle of Bubble and Squeak* (Puffin)

chapter 6
Ways of Working

Drama Modes

There are many different ways of working (drama modes) in drama. In the following charts I have tried to identify these different ways of working and look at the advantages and disadvantages of each. In this way we can assess the possibilities of each mode so that:

1 We don't expect too much from a mode that has obvious limitations;
2 We choose a mode that is accessible and manageable for the group;
3 We can use different modes for different purposes.

There is, of course, a certain amount of overlap between modes. Within a single session, we might use a variety of modes according to our 'readings' of the work being done by the group. But if our principle is to enable children to move beyond the surface of an idea, we will try to progress through modes that make *increasing* demands on the children. In shifting from one mode to another, we can take advantage of the overlapping so that the work *moves* along instead of jerking abruptly from one mode to another. It is important to try to keep a recognizable pattern going so that the group don't become confused.

An illustration might be useful at this point. A group of nine-year-olds have been reading *Elidor* by Alan Garner. They are confused about what sort of place Elidor is. The book offers few clues other than that Elidor is in the grips of the power of Darkness and its four sacred treasures are under threat. The only person mentioned is the lame King Malebron. To enable the children to clarify their understanding of this cloudy situation, the teacher works in the following way:

1 *Teacher-in-role mode* Malebron announces that the four treasures are to be brought to his castle under guard so that they can be displayed to the people and shown to be safe.
2 *Drawing mode* In four groups, the children draw a representation of their treasure (having decided that moving the 'real' treasure is too unsafe). Whilst they are 'fixing' their ideas about the treasure, they are also discussing why the treasure is important:

'Why should a cauldron be important?'
'Perhaps it stands for food, cooking and water.'
'Yes, and if it's stolen there will be no food.'

3   *Working in pairs (A + B) mode* Before they arrive at the castle, the guardians of the treasure talk with local villagers to discover whether there are any signs that things are not as they should be. They find out, and report back, that the nights are longer, there are no leaves because of the dark, mysterious shapes which have been seen at night etc.

4   *Whole-group improvisation mode* Malebron welcomes the guardians and their treasures. He asks what sort of journey they have had and what news they bring from the villages. Have they any explanation for what's going on? Each 'treasure' is then held up and Malebron asks each group to remind the others of the importance of their treasure and what it stands for – 'What might happen if your treasure was stolen?'

This illustration is offered simply as an example of a teacher using the charts on pp. 60–63 to help her decide on the most appropriate ways of working. The charts indicate the pros and cons of the modes *when each is used in isolation.* By relating and mixing modes sensitively it's quite possible to overcome (or compensate for) the cons, and also to reinforce the pros as well.

Drama Modes	Pros	Cons
1 Warm-Ups (physical) (See Clive Barker *Theatre Games*; Anna Scher *100 + 1 Ideas for Drama*)	Can 'gel' a class. Gets them moving. Releases pent-up or 'unuseful' energy.	Often inhibiting, considered childish by many children. Usually meaningless in themselves.
2 Games (See Donna Brandes *Gamester's Handbook*)	Useful initially to build trust/confidence. Icebreakers for insecure teachers/learners. Useful in restricted space or with 'wild' group. Rules are clearly defined and necessary.	Tend to substitute for 'the real thing' – quickly run out of ideas. Seldom require responses from the 'whole person'. Again, considered childish. No chance for reflection from within the activity.
3 Exercises (Acting, speech, thinking, gesture) Short, brief, teacher-controlled; specific tasks; or movement-based sequences of action. Teacher directs, often corrects, evaluates.	Useful as 'bricks' building towards the centre of the drama, for establishing technical points for later use, i.e. mime, tableaux, interview techniques; also as a starting-point for lesson, revealing existing attitudes and understanding.	Limited opportunity for discovery of meaning. Exposes individual strengths and weaknesses. Tends to result in stereotypic/clichéd work. Difficult for teacher to assess what's happening. Turns children into puppets controlled by puppeteer, unless sensitively introduced and a part of the overall context of meaning, i.e. there must be a purpose for the participants.
4 Mime Either individual or group, with or without speech, i.e. 'Pretend you're working in the castle, let's see what you do'.	Useful as 'business'. Helps younger children feel drama is 'real'. Encourages economy of expression, selectivity of symbol – can be powerful emotionally. Reveals nonverbal ways of communicating. Requires precision and children have some autonomy. Undemanding, relative to other forms. Satisfies children's desire to be	Abstract form. Difficult to develop without becoming too technical. Can be disorganized and messy. May descend into playground mimicry. Avoids the *real* demands to vocalize in appropriate register. Requires some techniques which participants may not possess.

5 Tableaux
Frozen moments, i.e. still pictures, solo and group.

Useful for introducing idea of images; focusses attention on a particular aspect. Way in to deciphering images. Encourages selectivity and economy of expression. Develops symbolic thought, awareness of spatial representation. Encourages discussion about meanings 'behind' actions. Stops action, giving time for reflection.

No opportunity for role development. Avoids interaction, particularly dialogue. Short-term specific goals. Lacks tension of an ongoing drama situation.

6 Drawing
(Drawing done during the session, rather than previously or afterwards)

Helps give credibility to situation. Establishes time and place. A familiar form of representation for children. 'Fixes' imaginative ideas.

An 'accessory' to drama rather than what it's all about – time consuming.

7 Writing
e.g. plans, letters, journals, messages, recording information.

Helps deepen response. Gives credibility. Writing as 'memorable speech'. Slows down pace of thinking. Writing for 'a real purpose', i.e. extending/affecting the drama. Encourages reflection. Quiet, meditative activity. Instrument for recording experience.

Introduction of writing seen perhaps as being indicative of the teacher's real priorities? Reveals individual strengths and weaknesses – gets in the way of action.

8 Showing Group Play
i.e. 'Make up a play in small groups about …,'

Useful for 'summarizing' work that has gone on. Social advantages of working together without teacher. Develops confidence and a sense of audience. Allows children to work as artists, i.e. finding shape and language for their own ideas. Useful to inexperienced teacher. Possibility of building up a series of related scenes to illustrate a single theme or development of an idea.

Children tend to show what they already know rather than discover new meanings as a result of improvisation. Tend to be stereotypic and clichéd. Problem of 'the loner'.

Work subject to peer-group pressures and attitudes. Danger of sexist/racist/infantile response. Difficult for teacher to intervene and shape ideas whilst work is in progress.

9 Interviews

i.e. media/local government/authorities etc.

Aids reflection. Useful in documentary drama. Reveals media-attitudes. Involves consideration of relevant questions as well as pressure of supplying relevant answers. Accessible/familiar form for children. Encourages serious response. Gets a response (in pairs work) from everyone. Possibility of perspective. Points-up contrasting viewpoints. Pressure of being questioned in-role – tests commitment.

Separates response from its c action. Difficult to articulate spontaneously without some pressure to do so. Need to be abilities of interviewer/interv as a means of recording what had already gone on. Difficult for teacher to control what is happening without breaking belief.

10 Documentary

i.e. presenting information about some topic (may include a variety of modes, e.g. tableaux/interview etc.)

Allows possibility of expert-roles. Encourages wider research and some measure of factual accuracy. Possibility of collage – approaching meaning in a variety of ways. Small groups contributing their own interests and enthusiasm. Consideration of forms of presentation. Useful as a teaching resource for other groups.

Often seen as 'assembly material'. Factual accuracy can swamp personal, intuitive response. Bits and pieces approach can be very confusing.

Few risks for learner or teacher – undemanding.

11 Simulation Situations

i.e. 'A is ..., B is ..., C is .... They are stuck in a lift – what happens?' (See John Seely *Drama Kits/Play Kits*.)

Very controlled, useful with difficult groups and inexperienced teachers. Particularly useful with 14+. Makes vocal demands without acting out. The teacher can control the situation and set its limits. Good for establishing different viewpoints, looking at registers and roles. Good starting-point for discussion. Focus is limited and defined.

Closed nature offers little chance for inventiveness. Outcomes tend to be predictable.

Reflection unlikely 'within' the drama.

Understanding of role limited to the particular situation.

Children 'rent' teacher's ideas rather than forming (owning) their own.

12 Meetings

Parish, village, tribe, local government, protest, experts, social workers, teachers etc.

Easy way of getting groups into role. Role as a demonstration of attitude/viewpoint. Possibility of teacher-in-role as chairperson. Structure of meeting – i.e. agenda, speakers, speaking through the chair – acts as a control. Can be dramatic: 'We *must* have a meeting about this!' Useful with different age-groups, i.e. nine to adult. Useful way of introducing a 'disturbance' into an established order, encouraging suggestions for dealing with disturbance.

Can be dominated by most vocal members of the group. Teacher-directed. Language tends to be discursive and formal. Static, chair-bound activity. Group often too inhibited to participate in such an exposed situation.

13 Whole Group Improvisation with Teacher-in-Role

(See Dorothy Heathcote/Gavin Bolton *Towards a Theory of Drama in Education*; Geoff Davies *Practical Primary Drama*; Rosemary Linnell *Approaching Classroom Drama*. See also Chapters 4 and 5 in this book.)

Closest way of working to real experience. Often best chance of discovering new meaning. Involves everybody simultaneously. Teacher controls from *within* the drama. Pressure of facing here-and-now situations. Creative partnership between teacher and group, shaping and crafting as they go on. 'The way of working in which participants are most likely to question, accept challenges, make decisions, realize implications, go beyond stereotypes and discover new depths of language – as a direct result of their involvement, in role, *within* the imagined situation.' (O'Neill and Lambert)

The most demanding and complex of all drama structures. Requires considerable expertise and experience on the teacher's part. Often frustrating for children and teachers alike. Requires ability to 'plan-on-your-feet'. Difficult to sustain after 14+. Tends to be dominated by group leaders unless careful. Teacher often gives up due to early lack of success.

References

BARKER, C. (1977) *Theatre Games* (Eyre Methuen)

BOLTON, G. (1979) *Towards a Theory of Drama in Education* (Longman)

BRANDES, D. (1977) *Gamester's Handbook* (Hutchinson)

DAVIES, G. (1983) *Practical Primary Drama* (Heinemann Educational)

GARNER, A. (1965) *Elidor* (Collins)

O'NEILL, C. and LAMBERT, A. (1982) *Drama Structures* (Hutchinson)

SCHER, A. and VERRALL, C. (1975) *100+ Ideas for Drama* (Heinemann)

SEELY, J. (1977) *Drama Kits/Play Kits* (Oxford University Press)

chapter 7
Theatre Form

The 'ways of working' outlined in Chapter 6 represent different ways of organizing work: they do not represent the whole nature of dramatic activity. It's important to be aware of the available modes and to pick and choose a mix that will suit your class and your shared learning purpose, but most of the modes need to be consciously placed within a context that is theatrical in form if they are to work. This does not mean theatrical in the sense of *The Pirates of Penzance*, nor in the sense of performance skills. It is the *essence* of theatre that we are looking for. From earliest times, theatre, like sociology, has sought to examine the nature of social meanings, i.e. what it is to be human – in this sense it is theatre as 'active sociology' that interests us as drama teachers.

It's important to realize that theatre (as an art-form) does not work exclusively through actors and text; it employs a wider system of meaning-making in order to evoke and communicate with an audience. This wider system includes *signs* given by register, spatial relationships, costume, properties, pace, tension, non-verbal signals etc. Together, these different forms of sign combine to create composite *images* that hold and resonate the meanings of the play. The image then becomes a focus for the audience's thinking and responding. In the same way the teacher, in drama, works towards images (concrete form) that will hold the abstract at the centre of the group's dramatic exploration. This image will draw upon a wide system of signs in much the same way as a theatre image does. Effective classroom drama is dependent upon the teacher's ability to find appropriate images for the group to work with. It is a process that Gavin Bolton terms *'imaging'* – by which he means finding a situation or object that will stand for the abstract notion that is to be at the heart of the drama. In this way, the abstract meaning becomes embedded in a situation or object: it becomes recognizable to the children as something that is 'real-life' with its own identifiable intentions and purposes. As a result of successful 'imaging', a child is able to grapple with complex abstract notions beyond the boundaries of his own experience. It is rather like a teacher choosing a particular story to help a class come to terms with a difficult theme or concept. The story is chosen because it resonates the theme and yet it also presents the theme in terms of a recognizable human situation.

The teacher uses the very elements of theatre that are normally the tools of the playwright. As the playwright focusses meaning for the audience, so the teacher helps to focus meaning for the children; as the playwright builds tension for the audience, the teacher builds tension for the children; as the director and actors highlight meaning by the use of contrasts in sound, light and movement, so does the teacher; as the playwright chooses with great care the symbolic actions and objects that will operate at many levels of meaning for the audience, so will the teacher help the children find symbols in their work. (Bolton)

The following basic elements of theatre-form also belong to class-room drama.

Focus

Much has already been made of the importance of focus to drama work. Without a clear focus, drama quickly becomes diffused and confusing. The most common mistake we make in drama is to try and cover too much ground in too short a space of time. Once you've decided on a theme or topic, you and your class must settle together on *one particular aspect of it only*: the aspect most likely to be understood and found significant by the children as a result of working in drama.

For instance, if our topic is 'Robin Hood', there are numerous issues we might wish to deal with. For the purposes of our drama we will concentrate on the single issue of 'What drives people to give up their families and homes to become outlaws?', or possibly 'How can Robin Hood be an outlaw to some people and a hero to others?'. We would choose one or the other as our focus – not both.

Metaphor

Much learning in schools is metaphoric in the sense that schools separate learners from the real world. Contexts for learning in schools are there-fore metaphors for real-life contexts. The same is true of theatre, because theatre imitates reality; it is composed of metaphors which *stand for* the real thing. Having decided on a focus, the next task is for the teacher to decide on a situation, image or context which will resonate the chosen focus for children. This exercise will usually consist of building some kind of imagined world for children to work in – setting the scene if you like. It needs to be familiar enough for children to be able to work with credibility, but distant enough from their actual experience for it to be stretching and new. (Some part of the consequent work might be comparing this imagined reality with the actual reality it draws upon, e.g. 'What did you think of those outlaws we just met – how would you have *really* dealt with that situation?''). For instance, in the Robin Hood example it could be that we start by setting the scene in the outlaws' camp. It is mealtime and as we sit eating, we are swapping stories about how we came to be outlaws. In that metaphor there is a meeting of familiar experience and new experience.

Tension

Tension works to sustain interest and momentum. It can also work to check action which is becoming superficial. It's as well to have some tension, related to your focus, ready for use during the session and prepared as part of your planning. A tension might be a conflict, both actual as in Robin Hood versus the Sheriff of Nottingham, and also conflict in terms of attitudes, interests, backgrounds, cultures, ideologies as in 'The Normans will never understand our ways' or 'The West was not wild, until the white man came'. This tension between opposed forces of some kind, its examination and resolution, represents the problem-solving nature of drama.

A teacher working-in-role may control the pace and depth of the drama by using *challenges* as tension – perhaps a challenge of a child's role: 'How do I know you're an expert? – Prove it to me', or to the group's commitment: 'The king is tired of your silence. Unless you can find your voices, you must leave!', or as a caution: 'Careful! How do you know it's safe to go on?'. The learning purpose of both kinds of tension described here is to create a carefully-sustained balance between motivation for action and possibilities for reflection. Sometimes a tension is needed to stop the action in order to expose the interior of an experience; sometimes, tension is needed to bring pressure on the participants to move the action along.

Ritual

Ritual, of one kind or another, forms an important part of our personal and social lives. We reveal ourselves through those rituals that have a regular place in our lives. Rituals tend to be either an expression of what we believe in – as in theatre, religious events, courts or funerals, or an expression of personal commitments – as in elections, initiation rites, allegiance ceremonies, oath taking, farewell ceremonies. In both cases, the normal ebb and flow of human behaviour is checked. Instead there is a deliberate shape, contrived and convention-laden, placed on behaviour. So for the duration of the ritual we are aware of consciously *taking part* in an experience and the significance of the experience is also consciously heightened for us.

From a learning point of view, ritual is important because it is usually a social or collective experience; and also because cultural activity of a ritualistic nature illustrates an underlying ideology. The rituals we engage in say something about our society, its ideas and values.

The value of rituals in drama work is that they ask for a commitment from the participants – 'Will *each* of you swear an oath of allegiance to our leader?' – and also they slow down the pace of action and, as a result, the pace of thinking – 'As we pass the pipe of peace, let each Brave remember the events of this day'. The slowing down in pace is like the slowing down of thought necessary for writing, which is itself ritualistic in many ways. The language of rituals tends to be more considered and selective than the language of more naturalistic moments in the drama.

Contrasts

... Dramatic expression *can only be achieved* through the six elements

    Total darkness – Light
    Total stillness – Movement
    Total silence – Sound

used in all the infinitesimal gradations and mixtures possible between these poles, which together constitute man's living environment. (Heathcote)

It's difficult at first to recognize the importance of contrasts to drama work. In a sense, there will always be an intuitive use of contrasts: parts of the drama will happen at night, parts in the day; some moments will be busy, some stealthy or static. But a subtle use of contrasts in order to enhance, even create meaning, allows the teacher to work as an artist in her own classroom. An artist consciously manipulates gradations of contrast in order to make meaning in an artefact, to evoke responses at an emotional and sensory as well as at an intellectual level. In drama work, contrasts can work in much the same way to give emotional intensity to the session and evoke an appropriate response based upon what is being *felt* by the participants. An artist also uses contrasts to create a rhythm that oscillates between opposing poles and which sustains and carries the artefact through. In drama work, the teacher uses her understanding of contrasts for the same purpose – to give shape and symmetry to the lesson, not in an explicit textbook way, but in a way that is bound up with the content of the lesson and the children's responses to it.

Such an understanding of contrasts, valid or not, only comes from working with them and reflecting on the effect of particular combinations and variations. But trying to think from the start in terms of deliberately shaping and creating the contrasts in a drama session will help you to develop your planning skills. Some examples of contrast might be:

1 *Being aware of levels* – placing leaders/kings on a block to create a physical contrast between the king and his people.
2 *Being aware of paces* – following busy loose passages with quiet, contemplative moments; anecdotes around the fire at night after an eventful day for instance.
3 *Being aware of voice* – using different tones, registers, language and volume according to circumstance – family meetings compared with village meetings, for instance.
4 *Being aware of the possibilities of light* – using available light sources to vary the working environment.

Symbolic Objects

We don't need props, costume and scenery for drama. Too much attention to the external appearance of the drama results in 'dressing-up' at the level of funny hats and funny walks. Drama ought to be, as Harold Rosen said, 'cheap as dirt' in the sense that it is born out of the imagination and it requires only time, space and people for it to happen. But selecting objects that can be brought into the drama as a focus for the group's thoughts and feelings can work well, particularly if we choose objects that have a real symbolic resonance for children – a peace-pipe as a starting-point for working with Indians for instance; a rejected doll as a small baby with no one to look after it. Some objects may also help children into role – a stick for a role of authority; a cloak for a king; a large book for a wizard. Dorothy Heathcote has usefully identified objects that have symbolic meaning for children and classified their typical associations. Here are a few examples:

Candle – security, calm, light, solemnity, faith, loneliness, knowledge, shelter, fragility, time.
Cloak – authority, travel, comfort, power, strangeness.
Sword – self-preservation, power, authority, conquest, ritual, honesty, justice, retribution.
Key – security, limitation, freedom, cordiality, opportunity, intrigue, maturation, punishment, discovery, power, privacy.
Fire – sun, destruction, life, cleansing, eternity, faith, hope, magic, protection, superstition, passion, radiance, comfort, anger, warmth.

Our purpose in using these objects (which may be imagined if they are not easily available) is to focus the children's interest and attention. It is important to remember to accept only one of the meanings suggested by the objects as a basis for drama work. If the context suggests that fire means magic, then stick with that. Don't confuse the issue by introducing all the other associations.

Time

Once a group enters the imaginary world of drama, the normal rules of time become suspended. Time becomes flexible and passages of time can be organized in a variety of ways to suit the group's purposes.

Children working on making plays without any intervention from the teacher often produce episodic narratives stretching over several days, weeks, even years with the whole thing organized as short scenes compressed into three or four minutes of actual time. The limitations of such an approach are clear. One purpose of drama work is to lead children to an understanding of what's happening at a *particular moment* in time. The problem for the drama teacher is how to work against a child's natural desire to move to what happens next (in order to create the space for him to reflect upon what's happening now!).

Unless it is necessary to do otherwise (i.e. you are creating a conscious contrast) drama should move *slowly* – slowly enough to allow the material suggested by the present to be fully explored and understood. The effect of such a way of working is to offer a fuller understanding to the child, an understanding that is *empathic* rather than intellectual.

Imagine watching a play you have never seen or read before. If the performers work too fast, you won't be able to make sense of the play: it needs to work at a pace that gives us the opportunity to take in all that we are observing. It's the same for a child working in drama. If the pace moves more quickly than her understanding, then she will gain little from the experience.

The one common mistake in drama is working too quickly. It's difficult for teachers to work to the pace of children's understanding. We are not used (because of the pressures on us) to allowing children time to discover what they need to know for themselves.

In terms of planning, the rough principle might be to operate the drama moments of the lesson at life-rate, or slower. In other words, each event unfolds at the rate it would naturally do so, unless you want to slow it down further. If you want to explore a series of events occurring over a time-span, then arrange your drama as a series of scenes with breaks in between for discussion. Avoid living through an imagined day in five minutes of real time; look instead at a particular moment in the morning, the evening, at night etc.

Space

Participants in drama move from place to place; they stand alone and they work in pairs and groups. Theatre (unlike other art processes such as writing, painting, music) occurs in time *and* space. An informed use of space in planning drama helps to give a physical shape to the session. We make use of the possibilities of space in our drama work for both *functional* and *creative* purposes.

Functional

1 What sort of space is available for working in? Is it too big, too small, too echoey, too cluttered? How far will the space limit my options? Has it any good points; does it suggest anything?
2 How can I best arrange this group in this space? This is a more difficult question because a lot depends on your tolerance and the nature and age of the group. Younger children find it easier to focus on what is happening if they are grouped closely together – particularly when listening. Older children prefer circles.
3 However you start, the participants will arrange and rearrange themselves during the session. You may decide on a progression: whole group – solo – pairs – small group – whole group. You may contrast shapes: close together, spaced about; circles, horseshoes etc.
4 Choosing the right arrangement and recognizing the strengths and weaknesses of a working space will considerably affect the quality of the drama. *Good ideas often flounder because of an ill-considered use of space.*

Creative

It's possible also to use a sense of space to enhance and deepen the level of the drama.

1 The space around can become different kinds of space, imaginary worlds which we enter and walk about in – a medieval village, a spaceship, the prairies, the jungle, a haunted house, a Norman castle.
2 We can use space to represent meanings physically: marking out on the floor the size of a monster; the significance of circles to Indians' lore; creating a distance between groups or individuals who are alienated from each other so that crossing the distance physically becomes a metaphor for the reconciliation of the groups (although it is important *not* to create two equal-sized groups, working apart, who are in *conflict* with each other – that's how fights start!)
3 Awareness of levels; using blocks and platforms; deciding who sits, who stands, who kneels.

Role

What we will be discussing here is a concept of role rather than the practice of role or the psychology of role, both of which are dealt with elsewhere.

The idea of role is central to both theatre and drama, because both seek to examine the nature of social life; and our social lives are partly reflected through the various roles we adopt or have put upon us. In my own social life I am a father, teacher, learner, husband, houseowner etc. In terms of material for drama work, what is interesting is how my behaviour is regularized by these roles. How do they determine my attitudes to events, and how do events in turn shape my attitudes? For instance, what are the social and personal implications of my being a teacher? I might put this differently by returning to Robin Hood, and asking how the role of leader fits in with the role of outlaw – how will each role affect Robin's thinking and subsequent action?

It's important to realize the kind of emphasis that is being put on role in this description. There is always the danger in both theatre and drama that roles can become separated from reality to the extent that they become crude caricatures with gross mannerisms of voice and gesture. Such caricatures are also often vehicles for prejudice – Sambo, dumb blonde, Hick Irishman, macho-man. What is important in drama is to identify more generalized, universally-recognized roles such as farmer, leader, traveller, tribesman, peasant, father, brother, guard etc. and to explore the personal and social implications of such roles. In other words, one purpose of the drama will be to help children understand what it is like to occupy these universal roles in the real world.

Of course, an understanding of universal roles may need to be approached through work involving more specific roles related to particular circumstances. At the start of a drama, a child may only be aware of particulars like a name, an age, an historical context, domestic and local conditions. But as the drama proceeds and the child has to operate within the limitations and expectations of her chosen role, making decisions and suffering consequences as she goes along, it is possible that her role may jump out of the particular context of the drama and become a role that has a more universal context and meaning. For example, the child who plays one of Robin Hood's merry men may, by the end of the drama, be led to a more universal understanding of her role; she may see that she is in the same situation as all those who live in hiding, who are persecuted or considered to be outlaws. Her merry-man experience leads her to an understanding of the outlaw experience – although of course this will depend on the depth of the drama experience and the teacher's ability to lead the child in role to a point of reflective awareness about her fictional situation.

Fig. 6 The role of Robin Hood: the particular and the universal

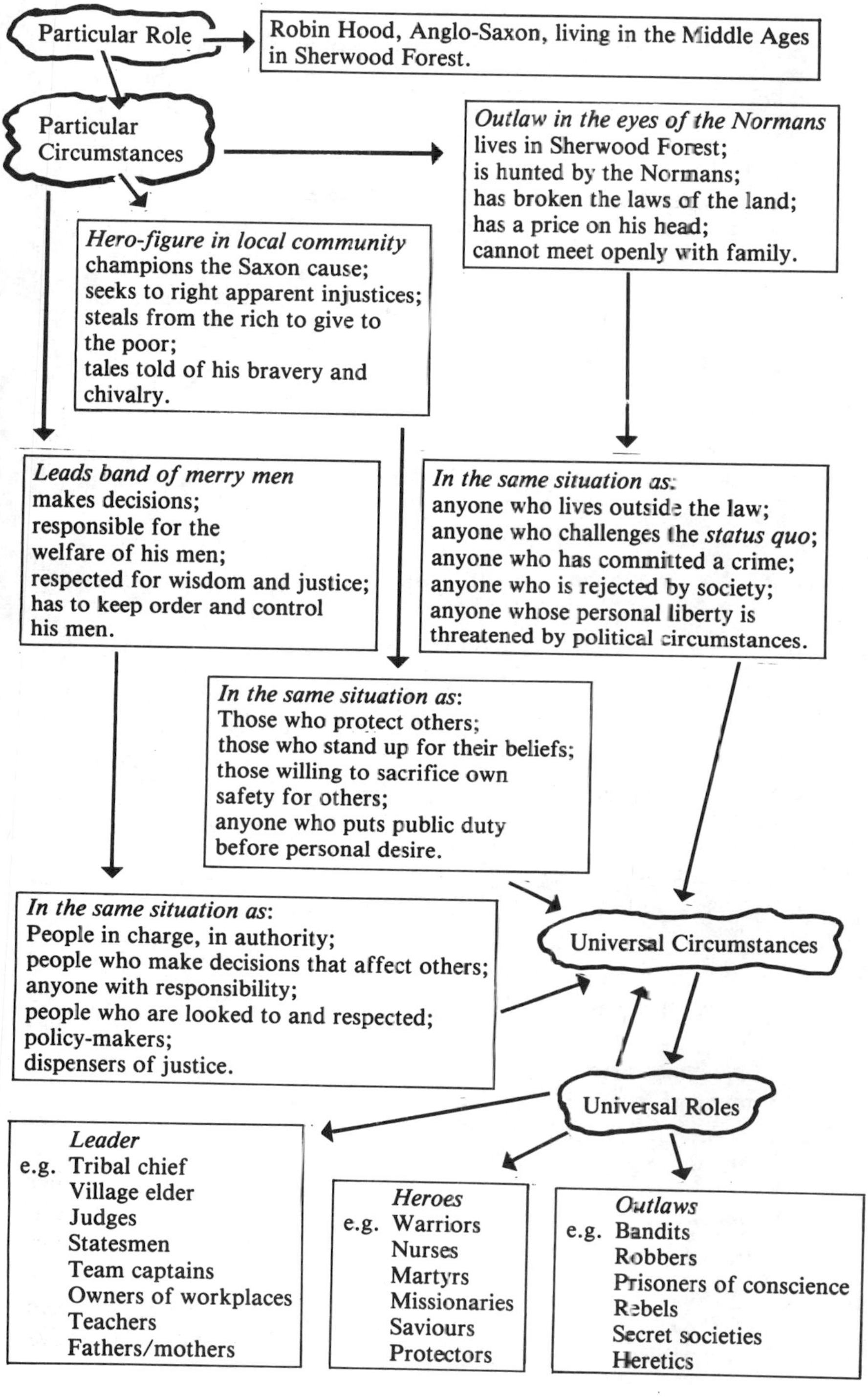

Particular Role → Robin Hood, Anglo-Saxon, living in the Middle Ages in Sherwood Forest.

Particular Circumstances

Outlaw in the eyes of the Normans
lives in Sherwood Forest;
is hunted by the Normans;
has broken the laws of the land;
has a price on his head;
cannot meet openly with family.

Hero-figure in local community
champions the Saxon cause;
seeks to right apparent injustices;
steals from the rich to give to the poor;
tales told of his bravery and chivalry.

Leads band of merry men
makes decisions;
responsible for the welfare of his men;
respected for wisdom and justice;
has to keep order and control his men.

In the same situation as:
anyone who lives outside the law;
anyone who challenges the *status quo*;
anyone who has committed a crime;
anyone who is rejected by society;
anyone whose personal liberty is threatened by political circumstances.

In the same situation as:
Those who protect others;
those who stand up for their beliefs;
those willing to sacrifice own safety for others;
anyone who puts public duty before personal desire.

In the same situation as:
People in charge, in authority;
people who make decisions that affect others;
anyone with responsibility;
people who are looked to and respected;
policy-makers;
dispensers of justice.

Universal Circumstances

Universal Roles

Leader
e.g. Tribal chief
Village elder
Judges
Statesmen
Team captains
Owners of workplaces
Teachers
Fathers/mothers

Heroes
e.g. Warriors
Nurses
Martyrs
Missionaries
Saviours
Protectors

Outlaws
e.g. Bandits
Robbers
Prisoners of conscience
Rebels
Secret societies
Heretics

73

As an example let us look again at Robin Hood, at the particular role which belongs to him, and then go on to consider the universal implications that might stem from that particular role, and how in turn Robin's role can be seen as connected to similar universal roles (Fig. 6).

In this chapter there has been a strong emphasis on the *experience* of a role, which leads to a crucial distinction between drama work and theatre production. In *drama*, the child has the possibility of discovering the implications of a role as a result of her involvement with it. The outward expression of her role may change considerably as a result of her growing inner understanding of the meaning of the role, revealed through the unfolding action of the drama. In *theatre*, the actor *starts* with complete interpretation of a role, arrived at through rehearsal and study of the text. His performance of a role will not change drastically during the performance unless such a change is indicated by the circumstances of the play: to be artistically 'true', his performance is expected to have a consistency of approach.

In terms of learning, the importance of this distinction is that as teachers we should be more concerned with the quality of the *experience* of a role for a child rather than with the quality of the *presentation* of the role. We should avoid directing a role's action and draw attention instead to what it means to be in a role. We don't want to spoil a child's chances by issuing inhibiting directives such as 'look like an old man', 'walk properly', 'speak up, the audience can't hear you'. Instead, we try to ask 'how does it feel to be old', 'how will you address your loyal subjects', 'what thoughts do you have at this moment' etc. In terms of learning possibilities, role-play as described here allows children to:

Try out someone else's shoes in fictional conditions so as to allow them to discover in safety what it must be like to *really* wear those shoes.

Discover that our own lives and the lives of other people are more complex and more interrelated than we imagine.

Discover new depths of language and registers released by unfamiliar roles.

Move beyond stereotypic understandings of role.

Interact with others in an 'as if' way without self-consciousness, threat or consequence (other than the consequences that occur in the fiction of the drama).

References

BOLTON, G. (1979) *Towards a Theory of Drama in Education* (Longman)

HEATHCOTE, D. (1979) Drama *Dance and Drama* Journal of the Leicestershire Dance and Drama Advisory Service

chapter 8
Drama Controls

It wouldn't be wise to suggest that drama is such a marvellous way of learning that the teacher (equipped with a well-wrought contract), will never face control problems, nor to suggest that particular forms of control will work with every teacher in every situation. The purpose of this book has been to suggest ways in which teachers can extend their own existing classroom practices to encompass the new dimensions of learning offered by drama work. In this chapter we will be looking at how the shaping of the drama session and the ways of working used in drama can help to extend teachers' existing classroom strategies for maintaining control. Three points will need to be kept in mind while you read this chapter:

1 Drama may present particular problems, but it is not inevitable that it will.

2 It is assumed that you have some confidence in dealing with routine control problems in your classroom.

3 This section is a guide to controlling *drama* work – the strategies looked at may not be generally applicable to other forms of learning.

Providing a Learning Structure Through Drama

When people first come to the idea of using drama in teaching there is sometimes the misconception that the activities involved will, by definition, be unstructured, uncontrolled, 'free', wholly spontaneous and potentially anarchic. This fallacy has several origins. We are still painfully conscious of the 'free expression' movement of the late sixties and early seventies which bred the naive assumption that given the right physical materials children could be left to their own imaginings, and as a result they could find form and shape for their ideas without the teacher's help. I hope it is clear by now that this book is not about ways of working that pursue this kind of recipe for chaos.

Another origin is the nature of the teacher-learner relationship in drama which is in some ways different from a normal classroom relationship. Allowing oneself to be vulnerable, shifting responsibility onto the group, dropping the natural authority inherent in teacher status, working in imaginary situations by adopting various guises and pretend roles is a scary prospect.

A further origin is the nature of the drama experience. It's easy to feel threatened by the prospect of working with groups in large empty spaces without the security of textbooks, worksheets and exercise-books. We have all been in the hall, pulling our hair out, whilst the group rush frantically about, clinging monkey-like to the wallbars and the head-teacher looks on knowingly.

The kind of drama we are concentrating on here is not often noisy or chaotic, nor is it intended to provide children with opportunities for free expression. It is seen instead as a means of providing children with a structured opportunity for reflection, interpretation, and thoughtful active exploration.

The intention here is to look at ways of preparing for this opportunity by creating *in advance* circumstances in which reflection, interpretation and exploration are going to be possible.

The Drama Contract

The first essential preparation is the setting up of a contract as a dialogue that respects the two sides (teacher-learner) of the classroom relation-ship. This contract provides the vehicle for looking at problems of control should they arise. If the drama isn't working we can turn back to the terms of the contract and see where we're going wrong. We can stop, and keep stopping, until it's possible for us to go back and carry on the drama.

It takes a while to appreciate that it is possible to stop and restart in this way. As teachers we often feel that once we start a drama, we must keep going no matter what happens. I am suggesting that whilst it may be desirable not to break the continuity of the drama, if necessary the drama must stop at the point at which a teacher feels insecure about her ability to control, or understand what's going on.

It's important to remember that for many children their closest familiar experience to drama is games. Games require rules in order to work, and the rules must be explicit, i.e. known and shared by all the participants. The terms of the contract have the same relationship to drama as rules do to games (although the terms will always be more subtle than simple rules are).

We must also remember that children have an ability to drop in and out of fiction without much loss of effect or concentration. We can interrupt and talk with them when they are 'lost in a story' in the class-reader context; and we can just as effectively interrupt them when they are 'lost in a play' in the drama context. An example here might help. A group of twelve-year-olds are working on a 'ghosts' theme. As they approach the doors of the haunted house, some of the boys start to whoop and laugh, making mock-frightened gestures. The teacher (caretaker of the house) comes out of the role and stops the drama. He tells the group that they need to decide whether they want to do a spoof-horror play or whether they want to work at a more serious and sinister level. The group agree to work at establishing more belief in the idea of a home that is *really* haunted. They approach again. It's starting to feel more authentic but some of the boys still have a problem. The teacher stops again. This pattern is repeated yet again but finally the group do approach at what feels like a different level from the previous work. Stopping and restarting has helped this group to become more involved in the drama.

Space*

Many control problems stem from an undefined use of space. We are used to the definition given by desks and chairs, and as a result there is a need for us to practise and refine other definitions (uses), of space. If we remove the desks and chairs we need to decide how else the space is to be arranged to suit the group's learning.

It's a good idea to have some routine use of space at the beginning of sessions, so that it's clear to a group that their use of space will be controlled. In a large hall it makes sense to limit space by gathering groups into a corner, or establishing a circle pattern so that precious time isn't wasted trying to gather individuals from all over the hall. It is as well, also, to insist on some formality in the intitial grouping – in other words not to start the session until the 'control of space' has been accepted by all. Fig. 7, p. 78, illustrates defined and undefined uses of space.

A classroom presents the opposite kind of space problems in terms of the effect crowding might have on control. I find it useful to define classroom space as shown in Fig. 8, p. 78.

In extreme cases it may be necessary to use space not to emphasize group unity but to isolate each individual so that there is no distraction or interference from others. This kind of control is achieved through the traditional command of: 'Find your own space, away from everybody else, and sit in it.'

Small-group work is less likely to become uncontrolled if each group has a defined space to work in and if territories are marked and observed.

---

*Although space is an effective control, it serves other important functions as well. This section needs to be read in conjunction with the section on space in Chapter 7, p. 71.

Fig. 7 Defined and undefined uses of space

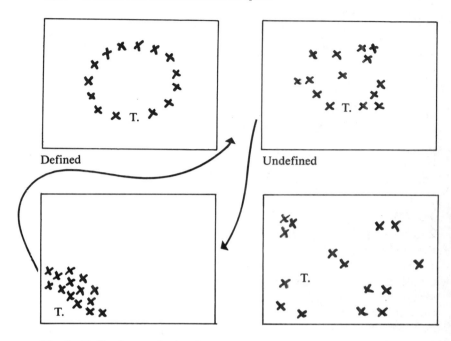

Defined   Undefined

Fig. 8 Defined space in the classroom

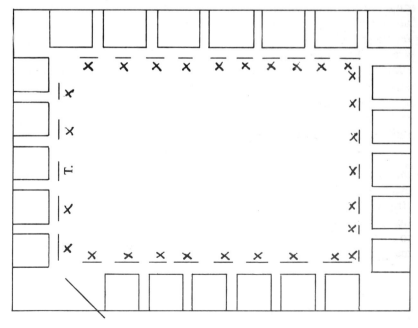

Role

Shifting into role means moving out of the actual roles that we have established for ourselves in the classroom, bearing in mind that from within our *assumed* (drama) roles we will still be consciously testing our *actual* roles. It's very seldom that a child will step totally into someone else's shoes – existing conflicts, strains, control problems, may still surface in the drama. But using assumed roles effectively can bring fresh and challenging control strategies into the classroom, in the sense that we are able to distract attention from our actual roles by assuming new ones, and also to view our actual roles from a different stand-point. If a teacher is concerned that a group's role-play should be authentic she might have to use the following strategies:

1 Allow only adult roles to be assumed – 'I am working with men and women, not boys and girls'.

2 Choose roles that carry a responsibility – 'How can the villagers trust the elders if they can't take our problems seriously?'

3 Insist on authentic attitudes and behaviour – 'Is this the way soldiers preparing for battle would behave?'

4 Select individual roles to help children with particular problems, choosing leaders, elders, lieutenants, foreman, messengers, experts, with care.

5 Use the need to share an identity as a means of drawing 'outsiders' into the drama – 'Are the rest of you willing to sail with these three if they are unwilling to perform the tasks allocated to them?'

6 Select teacher-roles with care, e.g. a leader – authority role with a group who require guidance and a sense of 'a teacher' being present – 'We are not prepared to speak with you until you learn how to address a king properly'.

7 Channel negative energies into opposition to teacher-role, i.e. if you're going to be anti, be anti me and what my role represents, (rather than be quarrelsome with each other).

These seven strategies are the ones that spring readily to mind; they may also reflect my existing experience of drama. I think that as we gain experience we get better at developing these sorts of preemptive strategies that allow us to control and develop the drama from *within*, i.e. we find ways of avoiding the kinds of control problems that force us to stop and resume our actual (teacher-learner) roles at moments which may be inappropriate to the true purpose of drama.

Rituals and Tests of Commitment*

Introducing rituals and other tests of commitment into the drama allows the teacher the opportunity to gauge individual interests and to remind the group of the commitment required of them generally. Rituals may be both ceremonial and secular and they require an individual contribution in a formal setting before 'witnesses'. Each child is being asked at one level to make a public commitment (however small or token) and at another to demonstrate the level of seriousness and belief each is prepared to work at. Here are some examples:

The king asks each knight to lay her hands on the sword as a mark of allegiance.

Each Indian brave reminds the tribe in turn how she received her name, 'I am called "Sharp Eyes", because I am a good scout for our people'.

The prospector asks the gold-dealers to pass around a piece of gold (imaginary) and to inspect it in turn.

Each immigrant produces a precious possession (imagined), and explains why she has selected it to take with her to a new life.

Newspaper reporters sent out to interview striking workers sit in a circle with the editor and report formally in turn.

Adolescents in a borstal answer to their names in a registration session.

A tribal meeting where only the person carrying the tribal mace may speak. Each warrior gives her own account of what equips her to go on a dangerous mission.

In a sense these sorts of rituals are symbolic of the contract-making that underpins drama work, and in the same way the ritual can become a focus for looking at any subsequent problems that may emerge in the drama. Rituals that test commitment remind the participants of what is required of them for the drama to work. Rituals that establish conditions of behaviour ask each individual to publicly accept those conditions.

Ways of Working as Controls

Different ways of working allow for greater or lesser direct control by the teacher. We need to remember that progress in drama work includes developing the ability to accept a shift from teacher-imposed discipline and forming of ideas towards self-discipline and self-mastery over the

*See Chapter 7 also, p. 67.

drama process. Chapter 6 looks at the opportunities for learning offered by various activities in drama. My somewhat reckless purpose here is to consider the various activities in terms of the amount of direct teacher-control implicit in each. It is a reckless purpose because I am in danger of suggesting the control element is somehow as important as the other purposes of each activity. It may be, however, that in a well-balanced and purposeful session you have to adopt one of the following activities for its control function:

teacher-directed exercises done solo
working in pairs (A and B)
games
meeting – where teacher has chair
tableaux
use of cards with information about roles to be assumed
teacher-directed movement sequences
writing
drawing
mime.

Choice of Material

The big advantage that drama enjoys over some ways of learning is that children have a natural enthusiasm for it. Unless they have been used or abused in the past, most children display a rare willingness to enter drama-time. So, as long as there is the trust that no one will be stared at without permission, or asked to perform meaningless and humiliating routines, or have weaknesses exposed, the child's expectation of drama is the strongest control the teacher has. It's interesting to see the group controlling disruptive individuals *themselves* in order to get on with an exciting play. (I don't often encounter this group pressure when I work with other ways of learning. But this inclination to drama must not be taken for granted – it needs nurturing.)

If a drama is well-conceived, the children's active engagement with where it's leading may become a powerful lure to be more involved in moving deeper into the drama. It might take a lifetime of experience to be able to negotiate dramas that never fail to stir a group, but you might find the following personal guidelines useful in gaining that kind of experience.

1 Never create situations where two groups are in conflict with each other. You may find that two plays, entirely different, run simultaneously.

2 There must always be a *tension* within the drama situation that turns

an everyday experience into a dramatic (not necessarily sensational) one – something that grips our interest. Dorothy Heathcote has a very precise analogy for marking this difference: Two male brain-surgeons discussing an operation, is not dramatic; two male brain-surgeons discussing an operation involving a woman they both love, is.

3   However alien the content, it must make some connection with something familiar to the child's experience (once again we are grateful to Mike Rosen and his list quoted on p. 5). This connection might not be a direct one but might instead be concerned with familiar attitudes, familiar forms of behaviour, familiar feelings – preparing for a long journey as a connection with the emigrants' experience, for example.

4   There must be something for everyone. If a sub-group become bored or sense there is nothing in it for them they will soon, understandably, become fidgety and negative. The teacher needs to plan for the variety of motivations and interests contained in her group. Some children may like to work with a friend rather than address a whole group; some may crave physical action; some may need to seek attention. If the teacher can satisfy this variety by blending different ways of working in her sessions she anticipates and diffuses control problems.

5   If an idea fails to engage the children's interest, drop it or reframe it in a different context. Working with a group of twelve-year-olds who I knew little about, I discovered that they were interested in doing a play about 'murder' and 'war'. A further stipulation was that there must be *lots* of bodies, not just one or two. After some preparation I addressed them as a group of ex-resistance workers who had been brought together to plot revenge on traitors who had betrayed their families and friends during the war. There was a stony silence, some sighs, disinterested stares; they were not going to take it up. We re-started. Six volunteers lay as bodies. I addressed the others as morgue-attendants on duty after a blitz and ordered them to bring in the bodies and itemize their injuries. Each group proceeded to produce their list – all likely bomb injuries – except for one group whose body had been murdered. Without a conference they were clearly signalling the play they were interested in doing.

chapter 9
A Planning Structure

You may find it useful to adopt a structure for your drama plans. Used flexibly and imaginatively, such a structure can prove to be an effective device for ordering thoughts and mapping out initial approaches; used rigidly and followed to the letter, it might prove to be disastrous! At least it might provide a way of ensuring that all the activities in a drama lesson are related and focus around a common theme or idea.

Considering Drama

In order to avoid later confusion, it might be as well to restate the conditions of drama which will need to be considered alongside the structure.

1 Drama is a development from child-play (games). It uses the same imaginative ability and self-control required in child-play, but in drama the imagined experience is controlled by the conventions of theatre as well as by the conventions of the game. The teacher is more likely to be aware of theatre (introducing its conventions to deepen the play/game), whereas the participants will be more aware of the conventions of game: taking turns, taking part together, not changing sides, observing the rules etc.

2 Drama, like child-play, implies working in an 'as if' or fictional way:

I am behaving '*as if*' I were this other person.
I am behaving '*as if*' I were in this situation.
I am behaving '*as if*' this object stands for something other than itself.

Often in drama the 'as if' will be in relation to all three.

3 In order to preserve a measure of psychological security for the participants, the situation and roles offered by the drama will be *clearly fictional*. Although the children will be exploring themes and issues which are familiar, they will be within a context that is 'removed' either in time or space from their actual situation and self. In this way the participants' actual selves are protected by the safe middle-ground of the fiction.

4   The participants should be always conscious that they are exploring a fiction, so that there is a choice of joining or not joining the game - a *willing* and conscious suspension of disbelief.

5   Drama is a fictional form, but it is not a narrative form - the purpose is not to engage with the make-believe at plot-level. In drama we become obsessed with what *is* happening *now*, rather than with guesses and speculation about what happens next.

6   Drama should seek to use something of children's existing experience, combined with their existing capacity for imaginative speculation, to explore unknown (or new) experience. In this sense, drama should be planned to *stretch* participants into new areas of learning.

7   Despite its fictional nature, drama should feel 'real' to the participants. This imagined reality may be more creative than factual reality, but it will observe some of the same rules, i.e. the drama will occur at life-rate (normal time-lapse); as in life, the drama will unfold without any preknowledge of what will happen next; it will operate within the limits of what's conceivable (i.e. it will not often be fantastic, or whimsical) unless it is otherwise desired; whatever conditions and conventions of behaviour are decided will apply to all participants - if you decide to behave 'as if' you are a group of village elders facing an important problem, then that's exactly how you will behave! If you decide to behave 'as if' your 'guns' shoot real bullets, if someone gets shot, they get shot!

8   In order to deepen the response of the participants to the drama the teacher will frequently enter the fiction and behave in an 'as if' way. She will maintain a responsibility and concern for what's actually going on, but she may well control the drama from *inside* the fiction, in her role as a participant. The teacher's purpose in entering the drama may be to:

challenge stereotype or easy answers
pinpoint the significance of what's going on
go against the *status quo* or group consensus
probe responses and press for more considered contributions
introduce new information
slow down the pace of the action
act as a catalyst for thinking and feeling by the participants
initiate new directions in the action
provide a model of appropriate language and behaviour.

Whatever role the teacher takes, she will be there as teacher (i.e. with a learning purpose in mind), not as performer.

9   Drama involves the emotions in at least three significant ways:

(a)   When we take on a role outside our own experience, one form of access is to consider the disposition associated with that role, i.e. the pride of a craftsman, the wisdom of an elder, the stealth of a hunter; these dispositions *are* within the range of our experience, even if the actual roles are not.

(b) As a result participants and teacher will present a type of person, rather than a particular person. They will demonstrate an attitude, rather than a character – but that attitude will have something to do with the situation and role they are reflecting on in the drama.

(c) The fiction of the drama evokes its own appropriate feeling response according to the level of the participants' involvement. This feeling response will be something like a reader's response to a fictional text (narrative): in other words, it may be powerful but it will be bound within the fiction and appropriate to it. The purpose is not to evoke feelings just for the sake of it – 'act angry', 'be sad' – but to explore the possibilities of the role and situation – 'How would you feel in this situation?', 'How does this situation feel to you? (i.e. your role)'. The point is that although drama works with *real* feelings, they are feelings evoked by the situation of the drama. They are feelings which are about something that is happening in the drama – they are not for effect or as a demonstration of how a feeling looks.

10 Working in an 'as if' way allows the participants to alter the existing dynamics of their group. The timid may become dominant. The dominant may become passive. The inarticulate may find voice. The able may find themselves struggling. It may mean that the teacher is able to shift the burden of leadership and decision-making onto other members of the group. She may allow herself to be *led* by the signals and responses offered by the group.

11 The overall purpose of drama in learning might be stated as 'to effect change'. Change, as a result of a drama experience, may occur in a number of dimensions:

change in level of understanding (a previous level of understanding modified as a result of the drama experience)
change in attitude
change in expectations of what role-play offers
change in social behaviour
change of existing language experience
change in awareness of others and their needs.

The list is not exhaustive, but it serves to show that drama requires careful evaluation. Useful drama will result in change; but it is not always immediately obvious in which dimension change has occurred, and indeed the dimension may differ from one participant to another.

A Planning Structure

Stage 1 Matching the group to the material

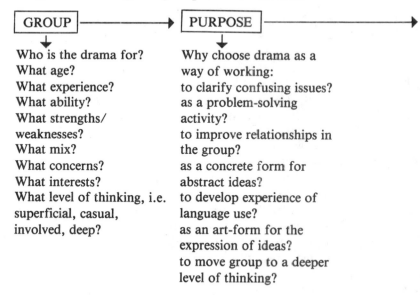

GROUP ──────────→ PURPOSE ─────────────────────→

Who is the drama for?
What age?
What experience?
What ability?
What strengths/
weaknesses?
What mix?
What concerns?
What interests?
What level of thinking, i.e.
superficial, casual,
involved, deep?

Why choose drama as a
way of working:
to clarify confusing issues?
as a problem-solving
activity?
to improve relationships in
the group?
as a concrete form for
abstract ideas?
to develop experience of
language use?
as an art-form for the
expression of ideas?
to move group to a deeper
level of thinking?

Stage 2 Establishing the dramatic context

The considerations of Stage 1, in particular the chosen focus,
will determine the practicalities of Stage 2, which are to do
with establishing a clearly defined starting-point for the role-play.

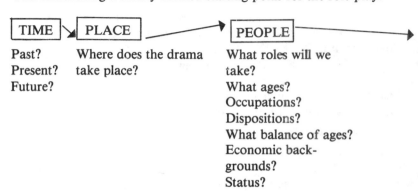

TIME ╲ PLACE ──────→ PEOPLE ────────────→

Past?
Present?
Future?

Where does the drama
take place?

What roles will we
take?
What ages?
Occupations?
Dispositions?
What balance of ages?
Economic back-
grounds?
Status?

| BROAD THEME | ⟶ | FOCUS |

Related to an area of
learning?
A particular story?
A moral issue?
Theme chosen by the
children?
New topic?
A human concept – such
as justice, kingship,
community?

Obviously you cannot
explore every aspect of the
theme, so what particular
aspect or key question are
you going to place at the
centre of your drama?
This will involve thinking
in terms of a generalized
experience and then
deciding on a particular
segment that is
appropriate to the group
and yourself (Norman
Invasion seen through the
more particular experience
of learning to live with the
invaders, for instance).
You may not find the *right*
focus at first – the ensuing
drama may demand a
different focus – but if
you choose your focus
with care, it becomes the
cornerstone for your
planning ideas.

| RELATIONSHIPS | ↗ | PROBLEMS |

What are the existing
relationships at the start
of the drama:
happy?
sad?
quarrels?
family groups?
individuals?

What is the motivating
force for the drama?
What is the initial
tension, or problem, to
be resolved?
What interests us about
these people, in this
place, at this time?

Stage 3 Framing the dramatic context
Defining 'frame'

Frame: in any social encounter there are two aspects present. One is the *action* necessary for the event to progress towards conclusions. The other is the *perspective* from which people are coming to enter the event. This is frame, and frame is the main agent in providing (a) *tension* and (b) *meaning* for the participants. (Heathcote)

Having established the particulars of the dramatic context, the time comes to make a start. At this stage the teacher will invite the participants to enter into the dramatic context through a chosen frame: she will try to find the most appropriate way into the learning material that is to be scrutinized through the *lens* of the dramatic context chosen by the group and herself. If the frame is right it will earn commitment from the participants and realize both the *purpose* and the *focus* identified in the earlier stages of the planning.

In planning frame three elements need to be considered:

What will be the form of entry into the dramatic context?

*The major consideration here is deciding on the degree of emotional distance you feel it is appropriate to place between the learning materials and the participants. You may decide that a particular theme is best worked on *indirectly* in order to preserve some sense of psychological security for the group (e.g. 'rape' or 'death'). Other themes might require a more direct approach. In the 'ghosts' example on page 89, there is a considerable difference between frames 1 and 4 for instance. A more extreme example might be the difference between putting children into a blacked-out room 'as if' it was actually a haunted place, and making puppets representing 'ghosts' who then perform a ghost-dance.*

With what viewpoint are we entering the dramatic context?
Again a consideration here will be the degree of directness you feel is appropriate. In the Beowulf example (p. 8) the children came at the dramatic context from a number of different points of view (implicit in the different frames):

1 as artists representing 'Grendel'
2 as figures in heroic tapestries of the time
3 as experts considering historical relics
4 as great warriors planning their mission.

What is the motivating force or tension?
Action implies movement and for the group to become involved there must be some sense (motive) of what sort of movement is required. What possibility for action is there? Why should we be bothered to initiate that action? Quite often the tension required may appear to the group, in the early stages, as a familiar game/tension:* needing to hide, needing to find, needing to escape, needing to win, needing to divert attention, etc.

Example 'Ghosts' †
Many different 'frames' are available for the children to make a productive relationship with this (or any) theme. The choice of frame by the teacher is crucial because some classes may find great difficulty with belief unless the frame is the right one for them. Many frames can be introduced or managed by a teacher in role.

Some such frames for this topic might be:

1   Children (hikers) decide to spend the night in a lonely old house. (Teacher-role: caretaker of house with stories of strange goings-on.)
2   Children (journalists) meet past owner (teacher-in-role) who pleads with them not to disturb the past.
3   Children (ghosts) scaring away the intruder (teacher-in-role).
4   Children as pictures that are able to speak of all the things they have witnessed.
5   Children as scientists writing their reports for the national Poltergeist Society (teacher is chief scientist, later a sceptic).
6   Children as detectives in their office provided with files on missing persons (teacher as chief detective, later as 'witness').

How Does the Structure Work?

As an illustration of the structure in practice, it might be useful to look at how a group of teachers used it to plan a particular drama.

Stage 1

Group
The teachers, who are from primary and secondary schools, decide on a mixed-ability class of eleven-year-old boys and girls in a city school. The class teacher is particularly concerned about aggressive antisocial behaviour in the group and a stubborn refusal, from some, to cooperate with one another.

*I am indebted to Geoff Readman for pointing this out to me.
†I am grateful to Chris Lawrence for this useful illustration.

Purpose

Accordingly, the teachers decide to concentrate on the behaviour and social problems within the group. They are looking for a drama experience that will require the group to work as a community and will place a responsibility on them for someone else's welfare and well-being. In particular they are keen for the group to consider what it *means* to work productively with others.

Theme

The children have themselves offered 'E.T.' as an idea to work on. The teachers decide that it's a good idea to keep close to the children's contribution for the following reasons:

1   to show that they are being listened to – their idea will become the dramatic context;
2   as a control. They have chosen the area, it is their responsibility to help the drama bring it alive!

The teachers, however, see little value in acting out the known story and seek to broaden out the area of experience to that of 'aliens', which has the same universal appeal as 'E.T.', but without the particularity of that one story. Most of all, they see 'aliens' as a way of exploring the universal experience of relating to an *outsider*.

Focus

After much discussion, the teachers offer several alternatives which they feel would satisfy the children's expectations of the topic whilst at the same time giving the teacher room to move beyond the surface of the topic.

1   Accepting, then helping an alien.
2   Modifying an evil/destructive alien's behaviour.
3   An alien outraged by our behaviour.
4   How to establish communication with an alien.
5   Alien threat to an established community.

Each of these ideas is entirely relevant and possible. Each segments the 'aliens' theme into something manageable and clearly defined. But a choice has to be made by the teachers. They decide it is best to decide now before they consider possible frames for the work. (In a different situation, they may have left the decision until after devising frames, or even until after work had started. Each drama requires a focus, but the *order* of the planning structure should help and not hinder – it must be flexibly considered.)

In drama we are often faced with decisions about ways of working and content. It helps to make a list of pros and cons for each alternative so that we can see what we gain and lose in each case.

PROS	CONS
1 Poses children with problem of how to make initial contact with someone from another world: Will alien be friendly? Will we be friendly? How do we signal our intentions? Helping the alien may help gel group into working together constructively.	May be some initial frustration in trying to communicate with aliens. Problem of establishing belief in idea of alien. If teacher takes alien's role, who will control and shape the rest of the group's work?
2 Children will have to consider their own behaviour in order to suggest a model of behaviour for the alien. In modifying the alien's destructive impulses they will be in the position their teacher usually occupies!	May react to alien's role in a similar vein, i.e. wanting to destroy/attack him. Such an approach may seem much more exciting initially. The presentation of the alien as evil/destructive may evoke hysterical/panic responses from participants.
3 Might encourage children to see their own problem-behaviour in a universal light, i.e. greed, war, exploitation. Might usefully broaden into a social studies context.	Children might see this as encouragement to behave in a gross and ill-considered manner. What role will children have? Being close to themselves might be risky. If a community, they might revert to their actual dynamics.
4 A sharply-defined focus on language, gesture, symbol needed to communicate intentions, values and signals to a being from another culture.	Avoids the main purpose of using drama for this group, which is to deal with existing problems in a fictional context. Also if alien is interestingly difficult to communicate with, some may become impatient and restless.

5 A good way of binding the group together to face a common threat. Provides a strong motivating force for the drama. Working on becoming 'an established community' may well be useful to this group.	Risk of hysterical reactions. Alien threat would have to be imagined if alien appears likely to be 'attacked'. Might encourage existing hostile/aggressive reactions.

The teachers decide to go for the first alternative, which seems to allow room for interesting possibilities. Rather than immediately introducing an 'alien' they decide to work on building the community and some general problem for some time before there is the *suggestion* that there may be an alien around. The children will then be left with interesting decisions to make: How do we find out what is causing the problem? Is the alien affecting us deliberately or unwittingly? To whom should we turn for help? How do we persuade aliens they are hurting us? What alternatives for help do we offer the aliens? How do we know whether to trust each other?

One important consideration at this stage is to resist physically introducing an alien role into the initial stages of the drama. This enables the teacher to work within the group as a member of the community, and also means there will be a clearer idea of what this 'alien' is like before anyone else takes on the role. The teachers also realize the danger of letting an 'us and them' situation occur with two groups working in conflict with each other. (In drama, it is as well to concentrate on just *one* group of people; otherwise, when you're working with the Indians, the Cowboys may decide independently to seize the time, rush over, and kill the Indians before your eyes!)

Stage 2

Time
The present.

Place
A small, isolated seaside village. (The group wanted a community that was self-contained, and the sea might offer interesting possibilities as well.)

People
Adults – a full spread of social roles, i.e. fishermen, mayor, shop-

keepers, farmers, policemen etc. (The teachers decide to sacrifice the child v. adult conspiracy element of 'E.T.'. Given the nature of this particular group of children, it seems a good idea to move them as far as possible from their actual situation.)

Relationships

Family groups, some existing feuds about fishing rights, some history of nets being cut, boats tampered with etc. (The advantage of family groups is to mix the sexes and create small units for decision-making and reflection. The teachers felt that initial work setting up family units would be useful to this group. With younger children, or a different group, they might have decided to work the children as individuals.)

Problem

The fish are dying; when the nets are brought in they are full, but the fish are dead. (This initial problem poses a mystery that may have a number of possible causes which can be considered before the teacher allows any suggestion of alien influence. In the back of their minds, the teachers are holding the idea that the alien craft is situated in the sea leaking radioactive waves into the surrounding waters – but it will be some time before they allow this idea, or a similar one, to emerge. Moving straight to the alien idea would be too easy a solution to the mystery – there are other possibilities to be considered first.)

Stage 3

Frames

The teachers decide to ask the children to establish their family units and some details about the village before initiating the drama. In different circumstances, they might have decided to start the drama, and then go back to establishing the family units. In this case, the teachers want to see the group *working together* before anything else.

Once the village is established, the teachers offer the following frames for the drama. (As an inexperienced group we prepared a list where the *viewpoint* was essentially the same in each example; there is a variety of *form* and *tension* however.)

FRAME	PRO	CON
Teacher in role appears as alien on the shoreline.	Introduces alien as a focus for the drama. Challenges the children to respond and enter the heart of the drama very quickly. There is a clear and strong tension to interest the group.	Children have no time to adjust to the fiction, i.e. who's who, what attitudes are present. They may not accept the teacher as alien; they might find an appropriate response difficult and adopt a comic approach.
Pairs in role of villagers discuss why there have been no fish lately.	Children can try out roles privately, i.e. not in front of everybody. Frame is likely to encourage an interesting variety of possible causes for fish-problem. Gives everyone a chance to vocalize straightaway. Easier to control than large groups.	Given the particular group, some may opt out and not enter the fiction. Less chance for teacher to challenge or deepen the responses or to assess the level of involvement. Avoids asking the group to act, and *behave*, as a community. Less chance to create tension within the situation: 'If there are no fish we will go hungry'.
An alien object is discovered in the village.	The object will make a good focus for speculation: 'What is it? Where is it from? What's in it? Is it safe? Why is it here?' The problem of how to deal *cautiously* with the object will slow down the pace of action.	May be difficult to prevent the group making impulsive decisions: 'Blow it up. Something's moving. E.T. go home.' Idea may cause initial discomfort for shy; might seem like an *over* suspension of belief!

| Village meeting called to discuss fish problem. | A comfortable, undemanding frame. Children are involved in fictional discussion, which they are used to. Chance to get used to roles. Children can get involved vocally as and when they are ready. Allows teacher to encourage a variety of responses and to question superficial contributions. Teacher is clearly 'in charge'. | Teacher too clearly in control of what happens. Pupil-to-pupil exchanges unlikely. Petty disagreements may divert from focus. Lacks the emotional atmosphere of the more theatrical frames. |

The teachers decide on the village-meeting frame as the best starting-point – it seems to match the thinking behind the previous stages of planning. But in selecting this frame, the teachers have given close consideration to several other frames which might also be used subsequently if the first frame misses the mark. It's quite possible to depict the same landscape in a number of different frames. Each frame will throw a different light on the material and make a different, or more comprehensive, understanding possible.

Exercises in Planning

1 You regularly work with a group of eleven-year-olds (mixed ability and gender) in the hall for an hour a week. Previously their work has tended to be frivolous. There is a small group of boisterous boys who try to dominate the group. In general you find it difficult to get the group to focus, or reflect, on the work.

You decide to ask them what they would like to do drama about and hope that (a) this will earn commitment from them and (b) you will be able to do something serious and useful with what they offer. They supply you with this list:

1 cops and robbers
2 army

3   pop groups
4   horror.

Use the structure to plan an appropriate sequence of work for this group based on one of the themes given.

2   You are to teach a reception class of nine- (or eleven) year-olds who have had no experience of drama beyond school plays and assemblies. They have just arrived at their new school and the first-year theme for these initial weeks is to be 'Myself'. You want to start straightaway by building their confidence and letting them get used to teacher-in-role and other strategies. What would you plan to do with them (either keeping to the 'Myself' theme or not – as you wish)?

3   The form-tutor of a top middle (or secondary third-year, i.e. 13 +) has asked whether you could help with some of the problems she is encountering. The group appear to be turned-off; they are hostile and offensive towards each other and don't appear to be concerned about anything. To make matters worse, a small group of girls are openly defiant and wield considerable influence over other members of the group. The form-tutor feels that your drama time with them might help. What will you plan?

4   The humanities specialist is keen to look at 'Gender' as a topic with twelve-year-olds. He asks you to find a dramatic context for exploring the abstract notion of 'The changing role of women in society'. In particular he hopes you might focus on a specific historical instance to illustrate women's struggle for equality. Use the structure to plan a sequence of work matching this material to a mixed ability and gender group.

5   You are working with a group of seven- to eight-year-olds. The group is experienced in working to *Let's Move*, and their previous teacher was keen on dance and mime. As a result they enjoy and show aptitude for this kind of work, but they are unused to working in groups, and find it very difficult to originate their own ideas and to make decisions collectively. Plan a sequence of work that acknowledges their previous experience but also moves them further along.

6   These exercises are related to examples we looked at earlier in the book.

Beowulf (p. 8*ff.*)
Having looked at the transcript, what is your 'reading' of the group involved? What do you feel about the direction they are taking? How would you build upon the work they have just done? Use the planning structure to order your thoughts and suggest some further frames for this particular group.

Outsiders (p. 34)

The group were strongly against the notion of the ex-cons coming to their village. What frame might you introduce to allow them to *discover for themselves* the implications (and consequences) of the attitude they have expressed?

Indian Tribe (p. 35*ff.*)

This group of nine-year-olds are beginning to stumble upon the richness and meaning of an alien society's rituals and symbol. How would you develop the work to enable the group to gain further insight into the life and customs of the North American Indians?

Reference

HEATHCOTE, D. (1982) Signs and portents *SCYPT Journal 9*

chapter 10
Some Lessons

I hope that these few lessons will be seen as an 'appendix' to the book rather than as part of its substance. They were developed to help inexperienced teachers and groups to 'try out' drama practice in confidence. The purpose of this book, however, is to help teachers and groups move on to the *next* stage which is to devise for themselves sessions that match their own particular needs and interests.

The weakness of these plans is that they are rather plot-orientated – they place too much emphasis on one thing happening after another. However, I am sure that creative teachers will overcome this weakness by chopping, changing and adding to the plans.

Of course we all have days when our energies desert us and we need to borrow ideas from others. These lessons may be useful for such days! A rather better selection of plans is to be found in *Drama Guidelines* (5–16) and *Drama Structures* (8–16), should you exhaust the examples given here.

There is a sense in which these plans stand in stark contrast to the understanding of drama expressed throughout the book. They sound rigid, deterministic; they are written as narrative instructions. Please do avoid following the plans blindly: introduce your own alternative frames; stay with bits that work; chop out sections you are not happy with; use the plans only as an *initial* starting-point for you and your class.

SLEEPING BEAUTY
(Five- to seven-year-olds)

Working together, working against impulsive aggressive behaviour.

1 'I know that you're all experts when it comes to fairy stories. I wonder what you can tell me about them? What do you expect from fairy stories?' (Invite suggestions about familiarity of the fairy-story form.)

'Would you like to do a play about Sleeping Beauty? How does the story start? Yes, yes, so it starts when she's born does it? And who was there?' (Remember, the wicked witch was not invited.) 'Would you like to be the good witches and wizards who are invited to the baby's christening?'

2   Individually children decide what they are going to be: the witch, or wizard, of the wind, of the trees, of the sun, of time etc., and what appropriate gift they are going to bring. Each child draws a picture of her gift and folds the paper so it is 'wrapped up', then goes and sits in a circle. At the centre of the circle, place something to symbolize the cradle, or crib.

3   Explain to the group that you are going to take the part of the king, or queen, and ask them how they will behave in the presence of royalty. In role of king, enter. Children stand and bow. Thank them for coming such a long distance and being so thoughtful as to bring presents. Ask each child to introduce herself to the others, 'I am the witch of the seas' etc.

Then each child takes a 'gift', explains what it is and places it under the 'crib'.

Ask if anyone has a special wish for the baby, particularly a wish that she will be good and not get into trouble.

Ask if the witches and wizards will solemnly swear to protect the baby against harm and mischief.

4   Ask the witches and wizards to move into the throne room as you wish to hear if they have any news. Group get up and move to another space. (This gives a chance to break circle and regroup less formally and time to consider what news they might have.)

Listen to the news, encourage elaboration of detail. If it's not suggested, ask whether anyone has heard about the wicked witch. Why is she wicked? What does she do? Explain that you cannot believe she's so awful. Will the witches and wizards act out very briefly some of the terrible things she has done? Form small groups to prepare examples and show them.

5   'What's to be done to prevent the wicked witch from coming here?' (Listen to suggestions.) 'Would it help if we put all our powers together to frighten her?'

6   The children might make better suggestions but if not, two ideas might be to make a fearsome dragon and to utter a corporate spell.

Dragon
(a)   In groups of three or four, join together to make a dragon shape. How will you move? What sound will you make? How will you

show that it is fierce and ugly? Stress the need for seriousness – giggling isn't scary!

(b) Look at the different groups' work, emphasizing the strengths of each.

(c) Work on making one huge dragon-shape, using all the members of the group. (Considerable cooperation is required, particularly when it comes to moving the dragon around the space. Control the pace of movement with drum-beats.)

(d) Practise putting the shape together quickly, in case the witch comes when they are asleep or seated around.

Spell

(a) Invite suggestions for the spell and put them together to make one spell, e.g. 'Abracadabra/hocus-pocus/alikazam/izzy-wizzy let's get busy'.

(b) Practise spell. Stand in an open circle, say spell once, advance into a huddled group, say once in a whisper, again but louder, and the third time rising to a crescendo at which the group spring up and scatter – scattering the wicked witch's power (i.e. similar form to a 'group-yell').

7 (You will have to decide whether the group will cope with the witch arriving and using the dragon and the spell to scare her, or whether it's best to tell them that their practising has scared her off.) Discuss with the group what should be done with the wicked witch. Argue that treatment like death, beating up, locking up, torture etc. would make us as wicked as the witch.

Arrange a meeting with the wicked witch (either yourself in-role, or another teacher), where the children try to persuade witch to give up being wicked. The witch might answer with:

But what if I like being wicked?
How else can I enjoy myself?
Sometimes I just have to be bad, how can I stop being tempted?
If I agree to try, can you help me?
Does anyone know a rhyme I could say when I'm tempted?

8 Try to find a suitable anti-temptation rhyme from the children's experience, i.e. 'Be good, be good, be good on your way/Be good, be good, be good every day.'

Stand in a large circle holding hands. The whole group is going to break their previous spell on the witch by chanting the rhyme three times. First time move circle around to the left, second time move circle around to the right. Stop, pause: 'I can feel all the goodness passing through your hands and entering me, I can feel my wickedness going away. Can you remind me what goodness is? Will anyone tell me something good they have done in the last few days? Yes... yes... yes... (etc.).'

Third time move circle around to the left! 'The wicked witch's spell is broken. She was never wicked again.'

THE IRON MAN*
(Eight- to ten-year-olds)

Exploring a text, working together, introduction to conventions of role and drama.

Part 1

1   Gather the children into a close group around you. Explain that you are going to be working on a story that may well be familiar to some (*The Iron Man* is a popular text). Explain that you are only going to read the first few pages and that you would like them to listen closely. If they like the sound of any of the words, or any of the images offered by the words, they should try to capture them and talk about them afterwards. Read the first few pages until '...night passed.'

2   Talk about words and images that the children offer. Encourage the group to offer their own anecdotes that connect with the text by asking questions like:

Have any of you been to the seaside?
Has anyone stood on a high cliff? What's it like?
Has anyone been on a cliff in a storm?
What happens to the sea in a storm?
What happens to the clouds?
Has anyone seen cars going off cliffs in films?
How tall is the Iron Man?
Is there any local landmark we could compare him with?
If his foot came crashing through the roof, how much space would it take up in here?

3   Split the children into groups of four or five. Give each group *one* piece of drawing paper and some colours. Ask each group to produce *one* drawing (but using everyone's ideas and skills to put it together) of the Iron Man standing on the cliff, or falling off it, or in pieces at the bottom. They should leave a space for writing their own description of the scene.

4   When the groups have finished, bring them together and look at each drawing in turn, indicating its strengths.

*Ted Hughes *The Iron Man* (Faber 1968) contains many ideas for drama, only a few are given here.

5 Ask the group if they would like to meet the Iron Man. Ask if anyone is willing to take the part of the Iron Man. (Choose carefully – the Iron Man will be mute, but under pressure, and needs to be alert to signals and cues.)

Place a block or chair at some distance from the main group. Explain that the Iron Man will stand on the block to help remind us that he is as 'tall as a house'.

Give the Iron Man a prepared envelope marked 'TOP SECRET. For the Iron Man's eyes only.' Inside are the following instructions:

You Cannot Speak
You Don't Understand Us
You Don't Trust Us
You Are Hungry.

Give the 'Iron Man' her sealed instructions, ask her to take them to one side, read them, and when she is ready, take up her position, in role, on the block or chair.

6 (During this section, you should position yourself behind the main group who are facing the Iron Man. This enables you to use visual signals to help the 'Iron Man'. Try to avoid talking to her directly as teacher, and also avoid letting the group in on whatever signals pass between you.) Ask the group if anyone has a question they would like to ask the Iron Man.

Choose someone to go forward and ask their question. (Remind himthat the Iron Man is a fairly frightening sight. He should approach with caution and treat her with respect. It is as well to remind the rest of the group that if they laugh, the Iron Man will be hurt and feel that they are mocking her .)

Hopefully your Iron Man will *not* answer or make any gesture. Do not help the questioner – let him be bewildered. Let a few others go and try with some more questions:

Well, he doesn't seem to hear us?
Has he got ears?
Oh, he doesn't talk, does he?
Perhaps he doesn't understand us?
How can we make him understand us without using words?
How do we show him that we're friends?
Oh, you think a handshake would work, do you?

Let someone go forward to try and shake hands with the Iron Man. (You may need to signal the Iron Man *not* to accept the handshake.) Let a few others try, then ask, 'Perhaps the Iron Man doesn't understand what a handshake means. What does it mean to us? Well, how can we show the Iron Man that? Are there two of you who can go up together and show him what a handshake means?' (When you feel the time is right, or unless she does so anyway, signal to the Iron Man to accept a handshake.)

7   Ask if everyone would like to shake hands with the Iron Man. Form a line some distance from him. Children go up individually, quietly and slowly, so as not to alarm/scare the Iron Man.

8   When half the group have shaken hands, get in line and go up yourself. Shake hands and whisper to the Iron Man, 'Don't shake any more hands. The first thing you are given: *eat* it.' Walk away. (It is hard on the next child when the Iron Man suddenly refuses her hand, but again let her be bewildered.) Let a few others try, then say, 'Well, we might as well go and sit down. He's obviously not going to shake our hands anymore.'

Sit the group down in their original positions.

Why won't he shake hands anymore?
Rusty?
Hungry?
Let's take him an oil-can./What does he eat?
Who will take it up?

(Whether the children decide he is rusty and needs oiling, or that he is hungry and needs a piece of metal, the Iron Man will eat whatever is brought to her, thus establishing that she is hungry.)

What other things would the Iron Man eat?
What could we find locally that he would eat?
Are there things in your house that he could eat?

Send the children off in pairs to collect whatever they might find in their own neighbourhood, bearing in mind that it *must* be something that two people could manage to carry/push/pull etc.

9   When the 'food' is collected together, explain that you are all going to try a guessing game. A pair stands and carries their object to another part of the room. As it is being carried the others have to guess, according to its size, weight, length etc., what it is.

10   Gather into a close group. 'Supposing the Iron Man didn't appear at the seaside, supposing he appeared somewhere near here – can anyone suggest a place where he might be hidden? Where no one goes? Where no one knows he's there?' Discuss various alternatives and finally elect a location. 'Supposing two or three of you found the Iron Man, who would you tell? Who wouldn't you tell? Why?' etc. Other questions might be:

Would you tell adults?
What would they do?
But what if they did believe you, what would they do?
Would it be safer to trust people your own age?

(There are obvious parallels here with E.T. which might be worth exploring.)

11   Ask if two or three people would like to find out what might happen at the police station if they took their story there.

Set up a police station with a desk, a few constables and yourself in role as the desk sergeant – a rather dismissive, harrassed-by-kids, no-time-for-stories sergeant! Beckon the children to start, and act out the scene with them.

12   Unless it has happened already, decide together which three people have seen the Iron Man.

How would they tell their classmates?
Without risk of being overheard?
Might other people hear them in the yard?
In class? Surely you don't talk and plan in class? Oh, you do?
Would it be an idea to plan a future, longer, meeting somewhere secret? Is there any place near here you could use?
When's the best time for a meeting, an exciting time?
Midnight? That sounds perfect. (!!)

13   Stand up in role as teacher. 'Right class, get in your places, come on, get your books out, start working and let's have no noise.' As teacher, settle class into their usual positions in the imagined classroom. Insist that they behave as they *normally* would, i.e. not in a comic-book way. When they are settled say, 'Right, now I have to pop out for a moment to see (name your headteacher). I don't want any talking while I'm out. You're to get on with your work. Peter, you're in charge and I want you to tell me if anything goes on while I'm out.' Move away from the group, through an imagined door which you close. (Some groups will straight-away huddle up and make plans quite spontaneously. Others might need reminding that this is the chance they have been waiting for.) When the group's talking starts to fizzle out, re-enter the classroom and ask the 'stoolpigeon' what happened.

14   Out of role ask the group what plans they have made. Perhaps they should have a password? Does anyone know a secret knock they could use? Try a few knocks out (try to get everybody knocking in unison).

15   Ask everyone to find their own space, away from others, and to lie down in it. 'Each of you will have your own problems getting out of your houses tonight. Perhaps you have a dog, a restless brother or sister,

creaky stairs, perhaps you have to climb down from your room. As you lie there, work out how you will get out without anyone noticing. . . . Now it's nearly time. You've waited for the house to go quiet, for the last light to be turned off, for the last light switch, for the last sound of voices. . . . Now you go!'

16 Whilst the group are busy escaping from their homes, arrange a limited space in one corner representing the meeting-place. Gather the group closely together in the opposite corner and whisper, 'Right, we're all here. Did anyone have trouble getting here. Yes, what happened to you? and you? OK, you've got to get across this open space into the meeting-place without anyone seeing you, give the knock and password and get in. Who knows how to do that? You go first then, and show us how it's done.'

Send the children off individually at first, then in small clusters. After a while, get up and, in the role of someone looking for a dog, enter the space calling out for your dog. Later on get up in the role of a policeman and challenge whoever happens to be crossing at the time – why are they out? so late? Run your torch across the hiding place to add tension.

When the group have all entered the meeting-place, withdraw, sit down and just watch. (The group may be confused by your absence at first, but if you're patient they will, hopefully, take the initiative and conduct a secret, whispered meeting between themselves.)

17 The children work in pairs. A is one of the children at the meeting, B is a brother/sister lying awake at home. Act out how A explains her absence.

Part 2

18 Explain that you would like to return for a while to Ted Hughes's version of the story. You will have to change some of the details in the previous work. Instead of the children being themselves, working in their own neighbourhood, can they imagine themselves to be a similar group living in the country, near the cliff in Ted Hughes's story?

What would be different?
What sort of jobs would your parents do?
What might the Iron Man find to eat in the country?
How would the country people feel about him eating those things?

Ask the group to set themselves up as if they were in school assembly the morning after the meeting. When they are ready, enter as the headteacher. 'Good morning. I am not at all pleased this morning. I have had Sergeant Pickering in my office since 8.00. He tells me he caught some of you out at . . . (name place where they met). I am sure you didn't have your parents' permission to be there. I want you to own up. Oh yes, he also says there were some strange heavy thudding noises near where you were, and coloured lights flashing – what was that? Does anyone know?' (Encourage responses that are excuses for the noise and lights – torches, dropping bricks etc.) 'Well, that's enough for now, but I shall be making some enquiries of my own; dismiss.'

19 If you have not already done so, read further on into *The Iron Man* – up until the morning after his feast of farm machinery.

> How do you think the farmers felt?
> What would they think caused it?
> What would they do first?
> Would they report it to the police?

Ask the group if they would like to take the roles of the farmers, gathering outside the police station. You will be the police sergeant. In the form of a standing meeting, deal with their complaints. (Try to keep them calm – you can't do your duty otherwise! Be business-like.)

> Now then, Sir, what exactly happened?
> Eaten, Sir? Do you expect me to believe that?
> This isn't an insurance swindle is it?
> And did you hear anything Sir? etc.

Send the farmers home, telling them that your constables will be calling on them to inspect the damage and take statements.

20 Split the group into pairs: A is a police constable, B is a farmer whose equipment has been damaged. In the role of police sergeant, send your constables off to interview the farmers.

When they have had time, call the group together. Sitting in a circle, explain to the Bs that you are only going to talk to the As and the Bs must not interrupt.

> Right, where's the first constable?
> And what did you find out?
> And what could have caused this damage?
> Could it have been an axe or a saw?
> Did you notice anything suspicious?

(Interview each constable in turn. Be fairly incredulous about stories of robots etc. Probe for a credible, 'understandable' explanation. After a while, you suspect that perhaps there is something very strange going on. You begin to appear rattled and confused by the constables' accounts.) When you have spoken to all the constables, tell them that you are very concerned and you're going to call in the experts – the army and the scientists.

21 Suggest that the group breaks into four separate groups of experts – army, scientists, farmers, children. Ask them which group they want to be in, then send the groups off to decide:

1 Is it possible that this damage has been caused by a giant robot?
2 Where could such a robot have come from?
3 What are they going to do about it?

When they have had time, arrange the groups in rows (on chairs, if possible) as if for a formal meeting. Invite each group to come forward and offer their views. Encourage the others to consider and debate the pros and cons of each view, reflecting their own interests as farmers, scientists etc. in the debate.

SPACE
(Eight- to eleven-year-olds) *

Responsibility of role, myth and legend; deepening responses.

---

1 Sit the group in a circle. Explain that your drama is going to be about the world and its future. Explain that although the world is comfortable and safe for us at present, it may be that in the future we will be less confident about its safety. Ask the group to give examples of things that might threaten the earth. Value every response, but look for ecological threats such as: pollution, exploitation of natural resources, deforestation, subsistence agriculture, nuclear waste, war etc.

Allow the discussion to go on long enough for you to establish a range of threats (they will not be articulated as specifically as they are in the list given!) and also for you to establish (without revealing a child's ignorance) the existing attitudes within the group. Questions for yourself at this stage might be:

Is it a problem that interests them?
Is there any emotional response to the issues?
Are there any misunderstandings, confusions?
Is there any conflict of opinion within the group?
How much do they already know?

2 Explain that you are going to start a drama based on some of the ideas discussed which is going to take them into space. In the role of a government official, say, 'I've been asked by the government to invite

---

*With eight-year-olds, concentrate on the physical action and organization parts of sessions. With older children concentrate on the discussion and negotiation parts of sessions.

you all here to this very secret, very private meeting, because you are all leading experts in your own special skill and have proved yourselves to be of value to the world. I have some news to give you, which I must ask you to keep secret. This news must not be told to anyone outside this room. The government has discovered that as a result of rapidly increasing pollution levels the atmosphere has been damaged. Ladies and gentlemen, the world has only five years left. In five years, it will all be over. However, since making this discovery, the government has spent all its money and resources on building the most advanced spaceship in the world. The spaceship's mission is to take a chosen group out into space to discover a planet where they can build a new world. When you leave this meeting, ladies and gentlemen, you must go away and decide whether you want to be considered for this mission. Remember that we will only take experts, and you must have a strong reason for wanting to join us.

3   After some talk about what sort of people will be chosen – what occupations, what characters etc. – the group go away and decide on names, occupations and individual *personal* reasons for joining the mission.

4   When they return, form an interview panel with yourself and two or three children (once they have qualified, of course!). Interview all those wishing to go.

And who are you, Sir?
And how will you be useful to us?
What sort of a nurse are you? Are you a specialist in space illnesses/ injuries?
And what's your reason for wanting to join us?

(Try to probe each child for more information about themselves without threatening the shy and inhibited.)

As each child is accepted, move them to another part of the room so that the accepted are a separate group from those waiting to be interviewed. (It is important to get the pace right so that it is neither boringly slow nor confusingly fast.) In a group of 30, interview 25 – then stop and count. Still in role, explain that the spaceship is only built for 25, unless, of course, the 25 are willing to have less space and so make room for five more who may have important skills that will be needed.

Are any of you willing to give up some space?
Will you mind living very closely together?
Is there anyone who feels unhappy about this arrangement?
Let's take a vote.

5   Explain to the group that they must go and say their final farewells

and that they can return with only *one* possession which will remind them of their old lives (the reason being that they have given up luggage space to take the five extra people).

6   After giving the group some time to consider which possession they are going to choose, split them into pairs: As are members of the space mission, Bs are someone close to them. How do As explain (sensitively) to Bs that they are leaving for ever and why?

7   Call the group into a large standing circle, and ask them to bring their possessions with them.

Can each of you show us what you've brought?
And why is your photo-album special to you?
Is there one photo which is more important than others?
Have you said goodbye to anyone special? How was that?
How do you feel now that we are about to leave?

(Depending on how much time you wish to spend, now is an opportunity to make space-logs, with a name, number, responsibility and space-badge on the front. Inside there should be pages for making notes and diary entries during the mission.)

8   Place the group around the room so that they physically represent the shape of a large, winged spaceship. Explain that this is what the spaceship looks like: storage is underneath, labs on top; in the front is the flight-deck and computers, in the rear is the medical bay, food and clothing; in the wings are the engines/armaments. The central area is the living and sleeping area.

9   Ask the group to suggest a suitable name for the spaceship, one that reflects the nature of its mission. Consider various suggestions and then elect one.

10   Ask the group to collect their things together and form groups so that the official photographer may record their departure. Pose each group in turn. Ask them to reflect their feelings about the mission in the way they group and pose. 'Photograph' each group.

11   'Right, let's get busy. It's nearly time for take-off! Check all your equipment! Make sure everything's packed away safely! Make your last minute checks! Medical staff, give everyone a space-jab! Come on, come on, there's no time to lose!' (Get the group moving, let them be fairly active, encourage them to be busy and quick.)

'It's time, ladies and gentlemen. Can you take your places on the special take-off couches? They are arranged here, in the centre of the ship, in a circle. Please lie on them so that your feet are all pointing to the centre and you are facing upwards.' (The take-off can be strengthened through whatever special effects you can muster.)

'I must warn you that the secret engines will take us faster than the speed of light. You won't feel or hear any mechanical noise, but you will black-out for five seconds.'

12   Countdown and take off. (You could indicate the black-out period with a click of the fingers followed by another.) Let the group get busy about the spaceship – checking instruments, arranging sleeping quarters, preparing a first space-meal.

13   Sit the group in a circle to eat the meal. As you eat discuss with them the problems they might face living and working together in the confined space of the ship.

> Should we have any rules?
> What will happen if there are arguments?
> If we can live together peacefully, will that be a sign for the future?

14   Settle the group down for their first night's sleep (lying in their take-off positions). When they are quiet you can say, 'This has been a very important day for us. Your lives will never be the same again. It could be that you find it difficult to sleep. Your minds may be buzzing with thoughts about the future and the past. As I walk past you, if you want to say what's on your mind, then you can speak and share your thoughts with us all.' (Walk slowly around the circle holding your hand out over each child.)

15   (This can be used if 14 is unsuccessful or as a reinforcement.) Explain to the group that their sleep was probably disturbed by vivid dreams about the future. Split the children into small groups and ask each group to act out the dream that one of them might have had. Give the opportunity for writing dreams and thoughts in the space-logs.

16   Sit the group in a circle. 'This is the first of several meetings we shall have during the mission. If we are going to set up a new world it's important that we don't repeat the mistakes that led to the destruction of the old one. It's important that we decide during the mission how we are going to organize the new world, and how we are going to avoid repeating mistakes. As the old world's experts, I wonder if you can identify what went wrong in the past...' (During the following discussion, try to probe and press the group to go beyond naive assumptions and to realize how difficult it is going to be to change old habits.)

> What went wrong in the old world?
> Greed? Well, what caused the greed?
> How can we stop people from being greedy in the future?
> But if we have no money, how will we buy things?
> Will you be happy if we all have the same amount?
> What if some people work harder than others? (etc.)

17   After discussion, carry on with, 'You are obviously going to need a leader in your new world. What special qualities will your leader need to possess?' (Discuss possibilities.) 'We have arranged a special test so that we can observe how likely leaders behave under difficult conditions. We are nearing the planet Morodor. You will of course be familiar with Morodor. It's well known as being a dangerous and evil place – spaceships usually avoid it. Perhaps those of you who have heard stories about Morodor could tell us of the dreadful dangers there.' (Make a list from the suggestions – man-eating plants, swamps, invisible monsters etc.) 'Several years ago a spaceship crashed into Morodor. It was carrying some vitally important cassettes. Your mission is to go down to Morodor armed only with a rope and a long stick, and retrieve the cassettes. You must work on your own, and when you return we will judge your leadership qualities on the account you give us of your adventures on the planet.'

Ask the clothing experts to hand out protective clothing. Explain that the group will be beamed down to a safe area; they do not have to go on an adventure, they can stay in the safe area if they like. Insist that they work alone without seeking help from others. The group then take up beam-down positions round the walls of the room. Click your fingers – five seconds – click and they're off!

18   When they return, sit the group in a circle and invite each child to stand in turn and give an account of his or her adventure.

19   Announce that the ship is about to move beyond radio-contact with earth. After this point, any radio messages will get to earth too late, so this is their last opportunity to send the last message ever from their spaceship. What are they going to say? Assemble the group around the ship's microphone. Let anyone who wishes speak their last words to earth.

WITCHCRAFT *
(Twelve- to fourteen-year-olds)

Establishing role-belief, moving beyond stereotypic responses, exploring community relationships.

---

1   Ask the group to sit on chairs in a circle. Start by explaining that you will be looking at witchcraft. 'I'll tell you a story about something that happened a long time ago in a village called Crookham. It was the year

*From an idea suggested by Cecily O'Neill.

111

1680, and at that time Crookham was a very isolated place far off any traveller's route. The families who lived there could trace their names back to the Doomsday Book. Being an isolated village, there were many superstitions, and some villagers practised country ways and followed the old religions that came before the Churches.'

What sort of superstitions might they be?
What do we know about witches?
What sort of people were accused of being witches?
Do you know about their medicine? About the wax dolls? etc.
What happened to witches when they were accused?

'In the year 1680 the witchfinder came to Crookham and began to hunt for witches. The villagers were gripped with a frenzy. Many were accused, some through jealousy and ignorance. Many were burnt and the smell of their burning flesh and the sound of their screams lingered in the air for many weeks after. A great shame settled on the village, and a great mistrust of outsiders kept away any new families.'

2 Read Beth Cross's poem 'Witch Spawn' from Roger McGough's *Strictly Private*.

3 'Now it's 1983 and we are going to be the parish council of Crookham. I shall be the chairperson.'

What is a parish council?
What sort of business does it do?
What sort of people would you expect to find on a parish council?

'Thank you ladies and gentlemen. It's been a very interesting meeting and we have concluded a lot of business. Just before we leave, there is one last item on the agenda. I've had a letter from a television producer at the BBC. He is making a series about English villages and he would like to know if we would be in favour of him making a documentary about Crookham. I wonder if any of you have anything to say about this idea?' (Encourage a balance between those for and those against. Press group to consider all the pros and cons. Be fairly dismissive about mention of witchcraft. Challenge with, 'Surely no one believes all those old wives' tales?') The meeting finishes with chairperson agreeing to write to BBC conveying mood of the meeting.

4 Ask everyone to work with a partner, and to go and sit next to this partner: As are researchers working for the BBC; Bs are villagers in Crookham.

Explain that the researchers' job is to go to Crookham and discover as much about the village and its people as possible. The people might be hostile to strangers so they must not arouse suspicion. They should try and meet the villagers in shops, pubs, on the streets etc. and get them talking. The villagers must decide for themselves whether they will speak to the strangers and what stories they will tell.

As and Bs go off and act out their meeting. (Stress the importance of concentrating on *what is said*.)

5 Collect everybody back into the circle. Explain that you will be the BBC producer responsible for the programme. Ask the Bs to stay out of the following conversation. 'Right, I understand you have been researching the village of Crookham. Can I hear from each of you in turn what you have found out?' (Go around the circle, hearing every A. Probe for more details, question whether certain stories are exaggerations, suggest further details – are there any unusual landmarks? what did you have to do to get them talking? etc.)

'Thank you, ladies and gentlemen. Can I ask you whether Crookham would be an interesting village to choose for our series? I think we should have another look to see what is going on. Are there four volunteers willing to go back to Crookham at night to snoop about, perhaps see what's going on inside the houses?' (Be careful not to choose the four strongest children – they will be needed for the following group work.)

6 Explain to the children that you want them to work in groups of four or five. They are to work on a piece of mime showing what the researchers might see going on in the houses at night. Each group must have a perfectly innocent excuse for their mime so that, for instance, a group of women writhing around a cauldron could also be rehearsing for a disco-dancing championship. Researchers observe groups working from a distance. Stress that precise, small movements may be more scary than comic-book gestures – an old woman rocking, stroking a black cat for instance.

7 When the groups are ready, collect them back into the circle. Explain that you want to re-create the chilly atmosphere of that night in Crookham, so you will see each group in silence and without a break. This means that when the first group finish, they return silently to their seats and the next group start. The groups should work within the circle. Number the groups and start.

8 Comment on the good points in each group's contributions. 'Now it's the following day. The villagers are at home and the researchers decide to visit them and challenge them about last night's activities. What excuse will the villagers give for their behaviour?' The researchers go to groups and question them.

9 Collect the group back into the circle. Explain that the parish council has called a special meeting and invited the BBC researchers to attend. Start the meeting.

'Welcome to our meeting. We know that those of you from the BBC are very interested in our village, so we would like to offer you an invitation. Every year on 31st October, we hold a festival in the church. The festival starts at 11.00 p.m., but the highlight is at midnight. Everybody will be there except the vicar – he always takes his holidays at that time of the year. You are welcome to come as our guests as long as you leave your recording equipment outside.'

Does anyone want to persuade the BBC to come?
Does anyone want to persuade them not to come?
What sort of festival might it be?
Why does the vicar go on holiday?
Do the BBC want to interview the vicar?

10 'We'll move ahead to the morning after the festival. One of the BBC men is found dead, without a sign of injury. The other three have lost their minds and cannot remember anything. They are taken to a hospital where specialists try to unlock the terrible memory that has driven them out of their minds.'

Explain that one group will work on a news bulletin about the dead BBC researcher while the other group will work as doctors trying to piece together the festival from the disturbed researchers. (Researchers will need advice from teacher on how to make the doctors work for information.)

References

HUGHES, T. (1968) *The Iron Man* (Faber)
McGOUGH, R. (1982) *Strictly Private* (Puffin)

THE APOTHECARY

(Nine- to twelve-year-olds)
To explore a moral dilemma safely, with the opportunity to discover the consequences of moral decisions.

The Issues

1 Teacher gathers group around board (or sugar-paper) writes SECRETS – OATHS – LOYALTIES invites anecdotal discussion around each, stressing that these three words will have a relevance to the drama.

What sort of secrets do we have?
What people do we have secrets with?
Have you ever broken a secret, how did you feel? etc.

What's an oath?

What oaths or promises do we use, when?

How important is an oath?

When in adult-life might you have to take an oath?

What sort of a word is loyalty – what does it mean – have you heard it used before?

Who do we have loyalties to? Brothers, sisters, parents, friends, family, country, Queen? etc.

Setting up a Village

2 Teacher explains that the drama will be set in medieval times. Teacher establishes that group has some knowledge of this period. What sort of buildings? Clothes? How would the village be different from today, occupations, travel and transport, customs and beliefs etc? The group's understanding doesn't need to be that deep at present. Their own existing understandings once collected together will probably be enough to work from. The teacher is trying to avoid too many anachronisms later in the play, by pre-empting them now.

3 Teacher asks group to suggest a name for the village. A rough map is drawn on the board. Is there a river? How many roads? Any special features. Is there a castle etc?

Teacher invites speculations about the range of occupations to be found in the village, stressing its self-sufficiency. Teacher explains that the most demanding role will be 'the Lord', asks for volunteers and selects boy or girl able to deal with the demands of this fairly central role. Each member of the group then decides upon an occupation – avoiding too many guards, cooks and servants and weak female roles – 'why not be a stonemason or miller?'

4 Group sits in a circle, teacher goes around asking each individual for details of her role. Talking to each 'as if' she was a villager – 'Ah, so you're the miller and do you make bread for everyone? Do you make cakes as well?' also establishing links between roles – 'Is the lord a good master? Does he make you work hard?' etc.

5 Teacher asks the group to use the space 'as if' it were the village and to show all the villagers busy at work, after allowing some time for the group to establish themselves the teacher stops the work and tells the group that she will shout 'freeze' after they have re-started and that she will come around and look at the village, and the villagers, to see what she can tell about the place and its people.

The group then resume work.

The teacher shouts 'freeze' goes round commenting on and questioning what's going on – trying to raise the status of contributions, filling in the gaps, moving beyond the surface of the group's action.

Is this a village where everyone co-operates?
Do you ever need help from anyone else?
Where are you going to sell what you're making?
There's a lot of cleaning going on, are you getting ready for a special event?
Do you just chop trees for firewood? Or is it for furniture as well?
Does the blacksmith just shoe horses?

(If the group are keen to be preparing for a special event such as the Lord's birthday – it will be useful to allow them to act-out some part of the event as authentically as possible to help build belief in the village. Perhaps each of the villagers bringing a present to the Lord.)

Introducing the Apothecary and his Problem

6   Teacher explains that there is still one person in the village left to meet. She draws a small house onto the village-map at some distance from the other dwellings. She draws a chimney with smoke saying as she does, 'the man who lives in this house is rather strange, he keeps his distance, he often locks himself away for days at a time – and all that the villagers see is peculiar looking smoke coming from the chimney – this man is the local apothecary'. The teacher writes the word on the board and helps the group to pronounce it. Teacher invites speculations about what an apothecary might be – settling for a definition that is part-scientist, part-doctor, part-wizard – some discussion on what sort of ingredients potions and medicines might include.

7   Teacher explains that when the play starts the villagers are most concerned because the apothecary has not been seen for over two weeks – people have seen smoke and heard noises, but they haven't seen the man himself. What might be wrong? Who should they tell?

8   The group assemble and prepare to go and visit the Lord to tell him and seek his advice. They knock at his door, are admitted by the guards and given audience. The Lord must decide what to do – go himself? Send his guards? Send the whole village?

9   Teacher in role of apothecary establishes a 'house' with a door. He awaits whoever has been despatched, when they knock he tells them to go away as he is too busy working on a problem – he must be left in peace. If the Lord comes himself he must obviously be shown some respect! The apothecary should make it very difficult for the Lord and the villagers to get him to the door to answer their questions – stressing he is busy, he has a problem, no-one can help him.

(He can dispense medicines through the door – getting the apothecary to open-up should become a problem for the group needing some imaginative strategies.)

10   Eventually the apothecary agrees to come to his door to talk to the whole village. He is obviously agitated and the villagers need to work at discovering what his problem is. *In other words the apothecary doesn't give all the following in one burst.* The group need to work for it. The apothecary tells them, 'I have a terrible problem, which I have been working on day and night for the last two weeks, and I can't stop until I have solved the problem. I mixed some herbs and flowers together to make this potion (holds up a bottle of coloured fluid). I have some rats in cages with various incurable diseases, I gave each some of this potion and all were cured. Do you realise what this means? This potion will cure anything. The problem is that I have forgotten how I made it. I have a friend who lives in a village two weeks' journey from here who would know how to analyse the potion, but it's too great a risk to travel there with this potion. I don't know what to do.'

11   The group of villagers will probably suggest a number of alternative courses of action – if they suggest going to fetch the 'friend' explain that he is very busy and very strange and he won't help unless you (the apothecary) go personally to visit him. They may suggest looking after the potion – explain that you are unhappy about that as it's a big responsibility – many people would be interested in stealing or buying it.

Eventually the apothecary agrees to leave the potion so long as the villagers swear an oath that they will protect it, keep it and not let a drop go. The villagers are asked if they are willing to make such an oath – the oath is solemnly made and the apothecary asks what punishment the villagers will accept should they break the oath. The villagers decide on how best to protect the potion, whilst the apothecary prepares for his journey.

The Moral Dilemma

12   The teacher explains that she will re-appear in the drama not as the apothecary but as a stranger. She asks the group to resume their day-to-day activities around the hall, she goes around asking in a loud voice for directions to the apothecary's house, when she has attracted everyone's attention she explains that she has come from Ashford, a village two days journey away. There is plague in the village, ten are dead and others are falling ill every day. She has heard that the apothecary has a new medicine, can she have some? The stranger needs to challenge why the villagers will not give the medicine over. Hadn't the two villages always helped each other? Did they realise people were dying? In the role of stranger, the teacher tries to initiate as full a debate as possible as to the pros and cons of not giving the medicine, with the Lord acting as chairperson. The stranger leaves promising to return when the villagers have had a chance to re-consider their decision. There should be some

opportunity for the kids to reflect upon the situation either in or out of the role. (Easy answers like 'Wait for the apothecary' and 'Come back in two weeks' need to be foiled by the teacher.)

13   The stranger returns and asks if the villagers have changed their minds. If they have not she produces an imagined bag which she says contains all the gold and valuables collected by her villagers, she allows the villagers to inspect 'the bag' and its contents. Are the villagers willing to sell the medicine? Again the stranger encourages a full debate and coaxes individuals to articulate their various points of view as forcibly as they can. *There must be opportunity for reflection, for reasons, for considering the moral dilemma the villagers are in.*

14   The teacher asks to borrow some cardigans. She arranges them so that they resemble a baby. She holds the baby, rocks it, and ask whether the group can believe in the bundle as a baby. If they can, the teacher returns as the stranger carrying the baby. She says that she has brought a baby who has the sickness. If the villagers still refuse to give her the medicine she will leave the baby in the village to die there.

Conclusion

The group are likely to be fairly hotly involved in the problem by this stage, they are likely to be divided about what to do. Confused about their loyalty to the apothecary. Scared by the threat of punishment if they break the oath. Worried that if they give the medicine away the apothecary will have none left to analyse and thus make more. I feel that it's too difficult a decision for the children to finally make in the drama. Best to stop and discuss the magnitude of the problem with the class. A further possibility would be to stage two alternative endings.

a)   The apothecary returns slowly towards the villagers who have given the medicine to the stranger. The apothecary forgives them, his friend has worked out the formula, he apologises for putting the villagers in such a difficult position.

b)   The villagers have decided not to give the medicine. The apothecary congratulates them on their loyalty but is distraught that others have died. The villagers may try to console him by explaining that at least many others in the future will be saved now that more medicine can be made. Perhaps the villagers will ask the stranger and other survivors to come and live in their village.

THE MYSTERIOUS HOUSE
(Eleven- to twelve-year-olds)

This session was devised for a group of eleven–twelve year olds with little drama experience. It was part of a project looking at mystery/ghost/horror stories as a genre. As such there is an emphasis upon the way in which these stories are constructed. The group had previously decided that the best stories revealed their secrets carefully and slowly over several pages – not immediately on the first page. This theme of 'not seeing too much, too quickly' was important to the session's construction.

1   The teacher and the group sit together in a circle, each member is given a clip-board, a pencil and some paper. The teacher explains that the play is going to be concerned with a mystery and that the group must be alert to any signs or clues that they are given in the play. Whatever role they take, they must also behave as 'detectives'. The teacher also explains that although the space is actually empty they will need to imagine they can all 'see' objects, rooms 'as if' they were actually there. The teacher asks them to agree to use their 'drama-eyes' in this way without letting others down. The teacher places two chairs to make a 'doorway' and asks the group to accept it as that. The teacher tells the group to wait until she has crossed over to the doorway and then to come over and join her. She explains that she will speak and behave 'as if' she is somebody else. She will give clues as to who she is, who they are and what sort of place it is.

2   The teacher goes over to the doorway. The group, armed with their clipboards, approach:

'Welcome to Darkwood Manor. My name is Harris, I work for the estate agents. As you can see the house has been rather neglected, prospective buyers have been rather put-off by its appearance and atmosphere. It's badly in need of a lick of paint and some fairly major repairs. Can I just ask how did you get here, did you come on a bus together?'

(The group responds, either by bus or other form of vehicle. The teacher indirectly indicates they have travelled some way by not allowing any foot-travellers!)

'You must have got a lift some of the way, and then walked from the village, I expect.'

'I'm sorry you have had to travel such a long way. We tried to get local builders and workpeople to come to the house, but none of them would. They all seemed to have some excuse for not coming here. Any builders? (Counts hands, if any.) Plumbers? Electricians? Antique experts (paintings and carpets)? Carpenters? (The teacher carries on until everyone has a role.) Right, well, we'll go in and let you make a thorough examination of the inside to find out what needs doing.'

3 The teacher stops the drama and asks the class to sit down. She invites their readings of the situation so far – What clues have been offered?

> What sort of place is it?
> What sort of person is Mr Harris?
> What will their work be?
> What will it be like inside the house?
> Why won't people buy the house?

Before resuming the teacher asks the group to piece together a collective image of what the house actually looks like – this can be done orally, in writing or through groups drawing a shared picture of the house.

4 The teacher begins again: 'Right I'll just knock and get the caretaker to open up for us.'

(The teacher knocks on the imaginary door. Waits, knocks again, during the following the group may suggest alternative forms of entry which if taken up by you might lead to interesting variations on the progression shown here.)

'Well, I'm sorry ladies and gentlemen, I can't understand it, he's never usually out – I feel awful bringing you all this way for nothing. I don't know what to do.'

(Again the group will have plenty of suggestions. The teacher here is firm that the front-door is the only access. The back-door is never unbolted. Whilst the group may peer through windows, they mustn't be broken.)

'Well I suppose I ought to find a phone and ring the owner, did anyone see a phone on their way up here? (Hopefully, someone will have.) Right. Well, I'll go and phone. What will you do while I'm gone? OK, I won't be long.' (The teacher leaves the group to explore the grounds and look at the outside of the house. She waits until the group begins to lose interest in the exploration then returns.) 'I'm sorry about that, Mr Stanhope, the owner says that the caretaker's son has been taken ill and the caretaker has gone to visit him. Apparently there is a spare key behind a loose stone in the wall. Did anyone notice it?' (Several hands go up, and the teacher asks someone to go and fetch the key.)

'OK. I'll open the door and then you can make a thorough inspection of the whole property. Make a list of everything that needs doing. Oh, there are two doors that are locked. There are no keys. Don't force them, just leave those two rooms and concentrate on the rest of the house. Leave before it gets dark.' (When questioned about this the teacher makes lame excuses about faulty electrics and following the owner's wishes. The group uses the whole space as the house and start to make lists of all that needs repair. The teacher moves around answering questions and offering encouragement. Eventually the teacher calls everyone together and ushers them out of the home with plenty of warnings about getting out before it gets too dark!)

5   Outside the house the teacher asks each group of workpeople to report on necessary repairs and observations they have made; deflecting anything too over-the-top. 'Those noises were probably the faulty plumbing.' Teacher explains that accommodation has been provided in the village, but they would do best to avoid the villagers and not to listen to gossip or superstitious 'country-talk' about the house.

6   The teacher stops the drama and moves the group into a different part of the hall. The teacher offers the group the opportunity to reflect on the work so far – firstly through a general discussion – and then by getting them into small groups and asking each group to prepare a list of five questions about the drama so far, e.g. Is the estate agent involved in the mystery? What's behind the two locked doors? When the small groups have compiled their lists of questions, they are read out without interruption. The teacher explains that the questions will help take the group further into the mystery. The teacher invites further speculation about the home and its mystery, encouraging a diversity of possibilities, beyond the obvious 'it's haunted' theme, i.e. 'It might be smugglers', 'The caretaker might want to keep the house'.

7   The teacher asks the group whether they think the builders would take any notice of the estate agent's warning about not talking to the villagers. The group indicate that they would not. The teacher asks the group to work in pairs; an A, and a B. A is one of the builders, B is a villager. The teacher suggests that some villagers may be reluctant to speak, some may exaggerate, some may be frightened etc. The pairs are asked to act-out their meeting and ensuing conversation. The group re-assemble in a circle. The teacher asks each A to recount the story she has heard and assess its credibility.

(If an interesting range of possibilities emerges from the villagers' stories, it might be useful for the group to work in fours or fives on representing different possible causes for the mystery 'as if' they were posing for an illustration to a story, i.e. as a tableau still-image.)

8   The teacher asks the group whether the builders would be put off by the villagers' stories, and whether they would leave the area and not bother with the house. The group indicate that the villagers' stories would cause them to go back after dark, in the hope of meeting the caretaker.

The teacher agrees to take the role of the caretaker. She asks the group to assemble as far from the 'door' of the house, as space permits. She spends some time asking the group to describe the appearance of the house and gardens at night, the manner in which they would approach, the nature of the fear they might feel on nearing the house. An agreement is made that the 'door' was to be the only possible form of entry into the house.

The teacher goes behind the door and beckons the group (it might take several attempts for the group to achieve an authentic response; there may be some nervous mock-horror spoofs at first). The group has the problem of a) getting the caretaker to speak with them, b) getting the caretaker to let them into the house. The teacher tells them to go away and is extremely suspicious and incredulous at whatever reason is given by the group for letting them in. She accuses them of tricking her out of the house; the son wasn't ill. She tells them to lower their voices because '*We* don't want to be disturbed' and that '*We* don't want you to change anything', she avoids any attempt to explain what is meant by we!

Eventually, she agrees to let three workpeople in as long as they decide which three for themselves.

9   At this point in the session the pressure to fulfil the mystery is very strong. The teacher either has to stop, draw together all the strands of the play so far and plan an outcome with the group; and then find a frame with which to explore it. Or, to act-out an idea she already has and reserve the consideration of alternative endings for later discussion/writing/illustrating. The teacher's idea for the drama is:

10   The caretaker surrenders and agrees to let the builders know the secret of the house. She asks them whether they will agree to be quiet and respectful when they enter the house. If they agree, the caretaker lets them in and asks them how they would behave in the presence of a ghost. (There must be agreement that there would be no manic hysteria even if it means stopping and talking it through.) The group are ushered into the corner of a room. They sit down. The caretaker tells them that it is nearly time and that the next person they see will be the ghost of Sir John Stanhope.

11   The caretaker returns as the ghost, she behaves normally but displays a nervous timid disposition. She says: 'I must check that my diaries are safe. I must make sure that no-one has unlocked the two doors and damaged the diaries. If only they were published I could rest in peace.' She sees the group and is obviously scared by their presence, she pleads to be left alone. The group are left to devise their own conclusion.